Eldest Daughter Syndrome

Empowering Big Sisters to Break Free
From Family Expectations, Reclaim Their
Identity, and Find Freedom

Jaylee Wade

© **Copyright 2024 - All rights reserved.**

The content contained within this book may not be reproduced, duplicated or transmitted without direct written permission from the author or the publisher.

Under no circumstances will any blame or legal responsibility be held against the publisher, or author, for any damages, reparation, or monetary loss due to the information contained within this book, either directly or indirectly.

Legal Notice:

This book is copyright protected. It is only for personal use. You cannot amend, distribute, sell, use, quote or paraphrase any part, or the content within this book, without the consent of the author or publisher.

Disclaimer Notice:

Please note the information contained within this document is for educational and entertainment purposes only. All effort has been executed to present accurate, up to date, reliable, complete information. No warranties of any kind are declared or implied. Readers acknowledge that the author is not engaged in the rendering of legal, financial, medical or professional advice. The content within this book has been derived from various sources. Please consult a licensed professional before attempting any techniques outlined in this book.

By reading this document, the reader agrees that under no circumstances is the author responsible for any losses, direct or indirect, that are incurred as a result of the use of the information contained within this document, including, but not limited to, errors, omissions, or inaccuracies.

Table of Contents

INTRODUCTION 1
    THE REALITY OF BEING AN ELDEST DAUGHTER 1
    THE VALUE OF READING THIS BOOK 2

CHAPTER 1 ELDEST DAUGHTER SYNDROME, EXPLAINED 7
    THE TERM AND IT'S ORIGINS 7
    HOW ELDEST DAUGHTER SYNDROME AFFECTS ELDEST DAUGHTERS 8
    IS ELDEST DAUGHTER SYNDROME A MEDICAL CONDITION? 10
    YOU KNOW YOU'RE THE ELDEST DAUGHTER WHEN... 12
    CONCLUDING THOUGHTS 14

CHAPTER 2 THE PRESSURES OF BEING THE ELDEST DAUGHTER 17
    THE SUPERPOWER YOU DIDN'T ASK FOR 17
    HOW PLAYING THE SECOND MOM SHAPED YOUR CHILDHOOD 18
    THE ELDEST DAUGHTER SURVIVAL KIT 26
    CONCLUDING THOUGHTS 28

CHAPTER 3 CULTURE, TRENDS, AND ON-SCREEN SISTERS 31
    BEING THE "BIG SIS" IN DIFFERENT CULTURES 31
    YOUR PLACE IN THE FAMILY MATTERS .... **ERROR! BOOKMARK NOT DEFINED.**
    MEDIA MYTHS AND MISSES ABOUT ELDEST DAUGHTERS 35
    EMPOWERING LESSONS FROM ELDEST DAUGHTERS IN POP CULTURE 37
    CONCLUDING THOUGHTS 40

CHAPTER 4 RECLAIM YOUR IDENTITY AND SELF-WORTH 43
    EXTERNAL VALIDATION VS. SELF-ACCEPTANCE 43
    EMBRACE WHO YOU ARE, UNAPOLOGETICALLY 44
    OVERCOMING THE IMPOSTER 46
    RECOGNIZING SELF-WORTH: BUILDING INTERNAL VALIDATION 48
    ELDEST DAUGHTER AFFIRMATIONS: PEP TALKS FOR THE EVERYDAY HERO 51
    CONCLUDING THOUGHTS 52

CHAPTER 5 NAVIGATING RELATIONSHIPS AND BOUNDARIES 55
    SIBLING RELATIONSHIPS AND THE POTENTIAL FOR FAVORITISM 55
    MASTERING NEGOTIATIONS WITH PARENTS 57
    BUILDING HEALTHY FRIENDSHIPS 58
    DATING WITHOUT THE DRAMA 60
    BREAKING THE RULES: WHEN THE ELDEST DAUGHTER SAYS "NO" 61

    Concluding Thoughts 63

CHAPTER 6 THE EMOTIONAL ROLLER COASTER OF BEING THE ELDEST 67

    Are You Feeling Anxious? 67
    Guilt: Handling Feelings of Unmet Expectations 71
    Shame: Exploring Deep-Rooted Emotional Responses 73
    Spotting Burnout Before It's Too Late 75
    Professional Stress Management Options 76
    Learning to Say "Yes" (to Yourself) 77
    Concluding Thoughts 79

CHAPTER 7 BREAKING THE CYCLE OF SELF-NEGLECT 83

    Rewrite Your Life Narrative 83
    Embrace Playfulness and Rediscovering Your Joy 87
    Cultivating Curiosity and Expanding Horizons 89
    Celebrating Individuality and Honoring Your True Self 92
    The Eldest Daughter's Playlist 95
    Concluding Thoughts 97

CHAPTER 8 UPLIFTING STORIES FROM ELDEST DAUGHTERS 99

    How Our Diverse Backgrounds Shape Our Childhoods 99
    Adult Sibling Shenanigans: Tales From the Front Lines 107
    Concluding Thoughts 110

CHAPTER 9 SUCCESS, REDEFINED 113

    Balancing Personal and Family Aspirations 113
    Creating a Vision Board for Success 115
    Creating New Family Legacies: Paving the Way for Future Generations 118
    The Eldest Daughter Bucket List: Things You Deserve to Do for Yourself 125
    Concluding Thoughts 127

CHAPTER 10 THE ART OF REFLECTION 129

    Get to Know Yourself Better Through Self-Assessments 129
    Setting Positive Future Intentions 132
    Speak Up: Continue Sharing Your Experiences With Others 133
    The Eldest Daughter Pledge 136
    Concluding Thoughts 138

CONCLUSION 139

ABOUT THE AUTHOR 143

REFERENCES 145

Introduction

She is water. Strong enough to drown you, soft enough to cleanse you, and deep enough to save you. –Adrian Michael

Go back in time and picture yourself as a child, gazing up at the world with wide eyes filled with both wonder and responsibility. You were likely not just a child but also a caretaker, a role model, and perhaps even a peacemaker. For many adult women who identify as eldest daughters, this scenario resonates deeply. Growing up as an eldest daughter often means stepping into shoes much bigger than your own from an early age, shouldering responsibilities that many people don't face until later in life.

This book is about you, the eldest daughter. It's designed to look into the unique challenges and pressures that come with this role. Such challenges are so common and yet so overlooked that social media users have popularized a term for them: *Eldest Daughter Syndrome*. This isn't a clinical diagnosis, but rather, a way to encapsulate the specific set of experiences and expectations that often accompany this role.

Eldest Daughter Syndrome refers to the emotional and psychological burdens often placed on firstborn daughters due to traditional family roles and societal expectations. These demands can start from infancy, shaping not just childhood experiences but also impacting personal and professional lives long into adulthood.

The Reality of Being an Eldest Daughter

There are a few things we don't get to choose about our life circumstances, and one of them is our birth order. Whether we are born first, in the middle, or last is simply the workings of fate. Nevertheless, once we are born, we soon realize that our position within our families carries some significance, especially when we have siblings. Eldest daughters, being first on the hierarchy, are often assigned unofficial duties that make their perspective of childhood different from their younger siblings.

From an early age, many eldest daughters act as "second moms" to their siblings. Maybe it was changing diapers, helping with homework, or mediating squabbles—yet, in some way, your formative years were closely tied to the welfare of others. Traits such as perfectionism, ingrained responsibility, and a constant drive for excellence tend to emerge from these experiences.

While these characteristics can be strengths, they also bring with them a heavy burden. The fear of disappointing family members or failing to meet high expectations can lead to anxiety and stress, leaving you caught in a cycle where balancing personal needs with family duties becomes an ongoing struggle.

Externally, cultural and societal influences add fuel to this fire. In many communities around the world, there's an unspoken rule that the eldest daughter must carry the heaviest load in family dynamics. Cultural norms, passed down through generations, reinforce the idea that eldest daughters are responsible for taking care of their parents and siblings, maintaining family cohesion, and providing ongoing emotional support (or, in some homes, even financial support). This cultural backdrop significantly shapes how eldest daughters see themselves and interact with their families. As these young women grow, they internalize these expectations, and this often leads to frustration and feelings of being undervalued when their efforts go unrecognized or when they are taken for granted.

The Value of Reading This Book

So, why write a book about this? Why focus specifically on the experiences of eldest daughters? Because understanding is the first step toward change.

The purpose of this book is not to moan about how difficult eldest daughters' lives are compared to their younger siblings. Even though this book sheds light on the complexities and nuances of being an eldest daughter, it doesn't discount the rich and meaningful lives that many eldest daughters live. Instead, this book seeks to provide clarity and validation for those who find themselves overwhelmed in this role and are looking for helpful strategies to cope. By investigating these patterns and experiences, we aim to equip you with practical tools that will help you reclaim your identity, recognize and respond to your needs, and navigate your responsibilities more effectively.

This book will serve as a guide for personal growth, offering insights on how to manage family dynamics while prioritizing your own well-being. You'll discover effective strategies for setting boundaries without feeling guilty and for asserting yourself in ways that foster healthy relationships. Moreover, you'll learn how to reach out to and connect with others who may be experiencing Eldest Daughter Syndrome too, building a strong community that understands and supports your unique challenges.

At its core, this book seeks to empower you. It aims to validate who you are beyond the confines of family roles and expectations. Often, eldest daughters put themselves last, focusing on everyone else's needs before their own. This book encourages you to flip that narrative.

Prioritizing self-care and nurturing your passions isn't selfish; it's essential. Through real-life stories, expert advice, actionable steps, and some light-hearted fun along the way, you'll find ways to reclaim your time, energy, and emotional well-being.

To all the eldest daughters reading this, know that your experiences matter. Your feelings are valid. And most importantly, that you have the power to redefine what it means to be an eldest daughter on your own terms. This book won't eliminate the challenges you face; instead, it will offer a new perspective on handling them, ensuring that you don't lose yourself while caring for others.

By the end of this book, my hope is that you'll feel seen, heard, and empowered to create a life that aligns with your needs and aspirations. You deserve to thrive, not just survive. As we embark on this journey together, let's explore the multifaceted world of being the eldest daughter, shedding light on its challenges and celebrating its strengths.

Welcome to a new chapter in understanding how to balance duty with dreams and responsibilities with self-care. Welcome to a deeper understanding of *you*.

"We cannot change what we are not aware of, and once we are aware, we cannot help but change."

Sheryl Sandberg

Chapter 1
Eldest Daughter Syndrome, Explained

The Term and It's Origins

Eldest Daughter Syndrome (EDS) is a term popularized by social media to describe the unique pressures and responsibilities often placed on the oldest girl child within a family. The fascination with EDS started in 2022, when a TikTok video (that has since accumulated six million views and counting) featuring licensed marriage and family therapist Kati Morton went viral (Luthria, 2024). In the video, Morton describes how EDS manifests and why so many women across the world resonate with the experience. Since then, multitudes of women have come out to describe the unique ways in which EDS has impacted their upbringing and adult lives.

Many people often wonder why this phenomenon is ascribed to the eldest daughters. To truly understand how birth order influences children's personalities and motivations (particularly young girls), we need to learn about birth order theory, a psychological theory originating from the 1900s, which was discovered by the Austrian psychotherapist Alfred Adler (Leno, 2024).

Adler suggested that the order in which children are born into a family can significantly impact their early childhood development. For instance, the eldest daughter might receive undivided attention initially, but then must adapt to sharing parental love and resources with the siblings who come after them. This shift often results in the eldest daughter gaining independence early on to play a supportive role to her parents, who may be overwhelmed with parenting and household needs. She may be asked to hold, feed, or watch over her younger siblings when her parents are busy or away. Without even realizing it, she assumes more responsibilities than are needed for a growing child.

Middle daughters have their own unique perspectives and experiences of childhood due to their birth order. They may not be required to take on a leadership role, but may feel overlooked in the family since they are neither the eldest nor the youngest. In other words, they may struggle to find where they fit in or what traits they need to develop in order to seek their parents' attention and affection. As a result, middle daughters tend to adopt people-pleasing tendencies as they navigate the waters of authentically expressing who they are and gaining acceptance from their parents to feel secure in themselves.

The youngest daughters tend to receive the largest portion of their parent's attention and affection because of their birth order. Even after reaching adulthood, they continue to be seen as the "babies" of the family. Like any baby, they are coddled and given more free passes than the older daughters. In some families, this unequal treatment can cause conflict and competition among siblings, with questions like "Why does she get to have that?" or "But why didn't she get in trouble?" being thrown around in heated family discussions. Compared to the eldest daughter, who is raised to be other-centered, the youngest develops a carefree, childlike personality, becoming overly focused on themselves and their own needs.

How Eldest Daughter Syndrome Affects Eldest Daughters

It's important to state, and perhaps emphasize throughout the book, that being the eldest daughter is not all doom and gloom. Many of the distressing experiences that we will unpack are often interwoven with fun and uplifting experiences. If you think back to your childhood, you may be able to recall memories of being an adventurous, experimental, rebellious person or the social butterfly of the family, immersed in your reality and loving every moment of it. However, with that said, being the eldest daughter did still mean growing up faster than your siblings and peers.

Studies have suggested that eldest daughters tend to mature sooner, both emotionally and physically, compared to their siblings (Miller, 2024). This accelerated maturity can be attributed to the additional responsibilities they shoulder early on, such as being the co-caregiver, organizer, and protector of their siblings, which leads to a heightened sense of duty and self-worth that is tied to their ability to manage family roles effectively. To some extent, you may derive some sense of satisfaction and accomplishment from being the one that your family members can trust and rely on. But when there aren't proper boundaries enforced to regulate how much you pour into others, your responsibilities can start to feel burdensome.

Another unspoken challenge that many eldest daughters face is the pressure to always have a solution for problems that arise within their family or friendship groups, even when they aren't sure what to do. Think about yourself for a moment. How many times have you said, "If I don't fix it, who will?" Feeling like a superwoman has its perks; however, over time, the pressure to bring solutions to the table can take an emotional toll on you. This could be the internal chaos of juggling other people's problems, plus your own, and giving yourself a hard time for not thinking of workable solutions quickly enough.

In many societies, traditional gender roles impose certain expectations on eldest daughters that younger siblings are not held up to. These expectations are rooted in historical practices where eldest daughters were often seen as second-in-command to the mother. While modern society is slowly challenging these roles, the aftermath of such expectations still influences how many eldest daughters navigate relationships today.

For example, if you had to be the strong one in your family to physically, emotionally, or financially support your parents and siblings, you may play a motherly role in your friendships, romantic relationships, and work relationships even today. Everyone from your local barrister to your colleagues leans on you for moral support. With all the emotional labor you do daily, you have already put in the hours for being a life coach!

The dialogue around EDS highlights a compelling need for greater empathy and understanding within families. Recognizing and alleviating the pressures on eldest daughters can lead to healthier family dynamics and empower them to pursue their aspirations without the guilt or fear of letting their families down.

These discussions can also help parents of young children address roles and responsibility inequalities from an early age. Knowing the long-term impact of EDS on eldest daughters, they can intentionally create an environment where all children, regardless of birth order, feel equally supported and valued.

The journey toward understanding EDS is ongoing, with each discussion adding depth to our collective insight. Future chapters will dive deeper into specific aspects of EDS and explore strategies to manage its effects. This foundational understanding will help you better navigate your own experiences or support loved ones who identify with the eldest daughter role.

Is Eldest Daughter Syndrome a Medical Condition?

EDS is not a medically acknowledged condition. As cited by Laurie Kramer, this syndrome is more of a colloquial term used casually in conversation rather than within the realms of medical or psychological diagnosis (Kayata, 2024).

The conception of EDS largely stems from anecdotal evidence rather than empirical studies. While it rings true for many eldest daughters who feel intense pressure to excel and manage family responsibilities, it lacks formal recognition. As a result of not being officially recognized, individual experiences can blur what causes EDS. For instance, diverse family structures and dynamics mean that not every first-born daughter will identify with the pressures associated with EDS. Some may find the weight of these responsibilities accentuated by cultural expectations, while others might thrive under similar circumstances without feeling overwhelmed.

Added to this, parenting styles can influence the likelihood of eldest daughters having EDS. For example, parents who are emotionally responsive and available to their children's needs may be mindful of how the family dynamics change with each child being brought into the family. They may involve their eldest children in some family planning conversations, allowing them to share their opinions and concerns about having younger siblings. When their siblings arrive, the parents may establish special times during the day when they bond with the eldest child to avoid making them feel left out or not a priority. Moreover, instead of all the responsibilities falling on the eldest child, the parents may distribute them to all the children according to their capabilities.

Middle children can also resonate with experiences similar to those described by EDS, which makes the notion that only eldest daughters face extraordinary family pressures far from accurate. Middle children's family roles often involve balancing between older and younger siblings, sometimes acting as peacemakers or negotiators within the family's complex social structure. These roles can lead to feelings of being overlooked or pressured to maintain harmony, illustrating that such challenges are not exclusive to eldest daughters.

Gender neutrality is another essential perspective to consider when discussing EDS. Eldest sons also encounter pressures similar to those attributed to EDS, which challenges the assumption that this phenomenon is exclusive to females. Eldest sons may equally bear the expectation of leadership, responsibility, and success within their families. The ideas of masculinity that are spread throughout our society add another layer, potentially increasing the burden on eldest sons to live up to both family and external expectations. Recognizing how, despite their birth order or gender, children can experience EDS allows for a more inclusive discussion about individual experiences within the family unit.

Therefore, instead of looking at EDS as a medical condition, it is more useful to see it as a social and psychological pattern that appears in some families and shape their interactions with each other.

You Know You're the Eldest Daughter When...

Being the eldest daughter in a family can often feel like being the CEO of an unruly startup. The role involves organizing, communicating, and problem-solving on a level that would make any corporate head proud. Yet, it's also filled with moments that are just plain humorous if you take a step back and look at them in a different light. Here are more unconventional ways to know if you have experienced EDS.

Organization

You know you're the eldest daughter when you take on the task of being the family organizer. You often find yourself in the role of the social director, meticulously planning family gatherings. Whether it's Thanksgiving dinner or a simple Sunday brunch, you morph into a seasoned event planner. It's not uncommon to see you juggling guest lists, dietary preferences, and seating arrangements like a pro. This role, however, comes with its perks. You get first dibs on important decisions such as menu choices and activity scheduling, subtly steering events to avoid your mother's infamous fruitcake or younger brother's karaoke disasters.

Communication

You know you're the eldest daughter when you serve as the communication hub. Imagine your parents being the board members who don't talk to employees directly, but rather, pass vital information through you, the CEO. Important updates, schedule changes, and the occasional sibling gossip flow through you as if you're operating the family switchboard. "Mom said to tell you dinner's at six," or "Dad wants you to come over on the weekend," become part of your regular vocabulary. The funny side? Sometimes, the messages get creatively "edited" or delayed to suit your convenience.

Conflict Resolution

You know you're the eldest daughter when you're called to be the referee in sibling conflicts. Picture yourself as a diplomat stationed among warring nations—that's how it feels when mediating sibling squabbles. Patience and diplomacy become second nature as you navigate through heated arguments about who's funding the next family road trip or who needs to apologize for making an offensive comment. In these moments, you channel inner peace, aiming to diffuse tension and restore harmony—often with a touch of humor. "Remember that time you argued over a Monopoly game and it almost led to World War III?" The ability to lighten the mood can defuse even the most intense standoffs, turning potential battles into shared laughs.

People Management

You know you're the eldest daughter when you carry a unique burden—the pressure to ensure everything runs smoothly in the family. It's like being the engine room on a ship, constantly working behind the scenes to keep things on course. This responsibility can sometimes feel overwhelming. You might find yourself double-checking everyone's schedules, preemptively handling potential crises, and even feeling responsible for maintaining family relationships. The pressure can lead to moments of frustration and exhaustion, but it also fosters resilience and strength.

Role-Modeling

You know you're the eldest daughter when you feel the responsibility to be the perfect role model. Your parents often expect you to be the shining example, setting the standard for your younger siblings. There's humor in this too—like when you catch yourself giving life advice, sounding eerily similar to a TED Talk speaker, only to realize you're barely keeping it together yourself. However, recognizing these expectations can help you develop a compassionate perspective. Understanding and acknowledging your limits becomes crucial. You learn to accept that it's okay not to have everything figured out and that asking for help doesn't diminish your strength.

True empowerment comes from recognizing that your worth lies beyond the family roles assigned to you. Being the eldest daughter is not just about meeting expectations set by others but about valuing yourself and your contributions. This empowerment fuels a positive cycle, encouraging you to pursue your passions and dreams without being weighed down by family obligations.

Concluding Thoughts

Eldest Daughter Syndrome (EDS) is a complex phenomenon rooted in family dynamics, societal expectations, and cultural traditions. This chapter has explored how a viral TikTok video amplified the awareness of EDS, shedding light on the unique pressures eldest daughters face. We've also discussed how Alfred Adler's birth order theory explains the roles of siblings in a family and how being the eldest daughter presents unique childhood experiences.

In the next chapter, we look at the societal and family expectations that create an invisible burden, affecting their emotional well-being and life choices.

"You are the one who possesses the keys to your being. You carry the passport to your own happiness."

Diane von Furstenberg

Chapter 2

The Pressures of Being the Eldest Daughter

The Superpower You Didn't Ask For

Have you ever been called the "second mom," even as a joke? You may have earned this title because of the many caretaking responsibilities that frequently fall on your shoulders as the eldest daughter. Unlike your younger siblings, you grew up being told to prioritize family obligations over personal aspirations, even if the message wasn't this explicit. It was normal for you to place your siblings' needs before your own and be there whenever they needed support. However, everyone has their physical, mental, and emotional limits, and sometimes, you may have felt resentment for always being the one people relied on.

The consequence of being seen as responsible and capable from an early age is that it shapes your identity and potentially causes you to mature too quickly. In many families, the premature maturity of the eldest daughters is seen as a testament to how intelligent they are. If you think back to your childhood, you may remember moments when you were praised for swaddling your infant sibling or changing their diaper all by yourself. While these are praiseworthy skills, they were signs that you were learning duties that were beyond your years.

Premature maturity negatively impacted your childhood development, too, as you skipped essential stages that small children, preteens, and teenagers go through. You may not have received enough play time, nap time, and free time to explore your interests because there were other people you had to look out for.

The label of being "responsible'" feels like a badge of honor in childhood. It's like being called a "good girl"—which young girl wouldn't want that? Later in life, being responsible can give you a head start in your college studies and career, allowing you to gain independence sooner than your peers. But at some point, the scales may tip over and your trait of responsibility could mean struggling to accept assistance from others or not knowing when to set boundaries. Socially, it could also lead to feelings of isolation, as you might struggle to connect with your peers who have not faced similar pressures.

While some eldest daughters embrace these roles out of love and duty, the incessant nature of such responsibilities can hinder their personal growth. Over time, the weight of these obligations can stir up feelings of frustration, particularly when their contributions go unnoticed or unappreciated by other family members. This resentment can further strain family dynamics, leading to conflicts and emotional distance between the eldest daughter and her siblings or parents.

An example of these dynamics can be seen in many households where the eldest daughter acts as a surrogate parent. In such scenarios, she might miss out on opportunities to pursue hobbies, educational goals, or social activities that her peers enjoy. Furthermore, seeing her siblings receive more freedom and fewer responsibilities can intensify feelings of unfairness and neglect. This uneven distribution of duties underscores the importance of recognizing and balancing family roles so as to prevent burnout and emotional distress.

How Playing the Second Mom Shaped Your Childhood

The scarcity of leisure time stands out as one of the most telling effects of heavy family responsibilities. Eldest daughters who spend the majority of their childhood helping out at home often have little time left for themselves. The lack of downtime can accumulate stress over time, manifesting as burnout when they enter adulthood.

The truth is, everybody has their breaking point, be it a parent or child. Understandably, the breaking point of a child comes much sooner than that of a parent due to their low stress tolerance. As you can imagine, the constant demands placed on eldest daughters overshadow their mental wellness, which can lead to long-term emotional repercussions. As they grow older and transition into adult roles, the continuous cycle of duty and responsibility can result in chronic stress and feelings of exhaustion.

Unlike the younger ones, the eldest child is assigned leadership roles. Despite the occasional perks, like being consulted first by their parents or having more decision-making power among their siblings, there are many unspoken sacrifices they need to make. One major sacrifice has to do with how they manage their time and organize priorities. Eldest daughters tend to prioritize the needs of others before their own and structure their lives accordingly. As the "responsible one" whom the family counts on, every decision is an opportunity to prove their devotion to others.

Balancing family expectations with maintaining relationships with peers creates another layer of complexity for eldest daughters. While their peers are engaging in social activities, exploring friendships, and building networks outside of the family, they may find themselves tethered to home obligations, leading to social alienation. For instance, declining invitations to social gatherings because of family duties not only deprives them of peer interaction but also isolates them from shared experiences that are pivotal during adolescence. Over time, this isolation can hinder their ability to form lasting connections, compounding feelings of loneliness and emotional detachment.

As eldest daughters move into adulthood, the struggle for independence remains a persistent challenge. The ingrained sense of responsibility and the expectation to prioritize family needs over personal aspirations continue to stifle their personal freedom. These deep-rooted duties often clash with their desire to forge an independent identity. Even as adults, many eldest daughters find it hard to break free from the role they've always known, perpetuating a cycle where family expectations continually compromise personal growth.

Take a moment to reflect on your life and weigh the impact of your missed childhood experiences, the lack of leisure time and social conflicts, and your restricted independence, which has now shaped your psychological landscape. What kinds of coping mechanisms have you developed over time to mitigate these pressures? Have you become someone who focuses on work and neglects their health or social life? Have you adopted rigid boundaries that make it hard for you to let your hair down, enjoy downtime, or form bonds with others? Do you find that you prioritize efficiency and task management over emotional well-being?

The expectation you place on yourself to be constantly available and capable sets a high bar that can be mentally taxing, leading to anxiety and depression. Moreover, the internalized pressure to meet these high expectations without complaint further exacerbates these issues, leaving little room for vulnerability or self-care.

In understanding the weight of these expectations, it's crucial to consider the broader implications for your overall development. The responsibilities thrust upon you can not only affect your immediate well-being but also have a lasting impact on your life choices and opportunities. The compounded pressures can—if left unaddressed—stunt your ability to take risks, pursue ambitions, and fully explore your potential outside the confines of family duties. Validating your experiences and opening yourself to receive support becomes vital in helping you manage your roles effectively while carving out space for your own growth and fulfillment.

The Struggle for Perfection

Caught up in the intricate web of family and social expectations, eldest daughters often find themselves shackled to a relentless pursuit of perfectionism. This tendency to chase flawless standards is not merely an isolated trait but, rather, a coping mechanism developed in response to the weighty expectations placed upon them. For many eldest daughters, the pursuit of perfectionism begins early in life, as they are often held up as paragons within their families, expected to set impeccable examples for younger siblings. The pressure to meet these high standards can be overwhelming, leading to chronic stress and anxiety that follows them into adulthood.

One significant consequence of this perfectionism is the perpetual fear of judgment. Eldest daughters frequently feel the need to project an image of competence and flawlessness to avoid criticism from family and peers. This constant fear inhibits their ability to be open and vulnerable, creating a facade that can be exhausting to maintain. The pressure to appear perfect can become so ingrained that it affects their interactions outside the family circle as well, limiting genuine connections and stifling emotional expression.

Even when they achieve significant milestones or accomplishments, many eldest daughters wrestle with imposter syndrome. This condition causes them to attribute their successes to luck rather than their skills or hard work. They may continuously feel like frauds, believing that at any moment, their perceived inadequacies will be exposed. This mindset not only undermines their self-esteem but also hampers their professional growth and personal fulfillment. The cycle of success followed by self-doubt becomes a persistent source of inner turmoil.

Winning the Battle With Your Inner Critic

If you have ever fallen into the trap of perfectionism, you know firsthand how relentless your inner critic can be when it points out every perceived mistake and magnifies it to make you feel small or incapable. Your inner critic might target specific aspects of your life where you feel the pressure to prove yourself, such as your career, academic standing, financial status, or family obligations. Thereafter, you might establish personal standards in these areas of your life that initially feel inspiring but later reveal themselves to be oppressive.

The relentless pursuit of your impossibly high standards creates an environment where relaxation and enjoyment become virtually impossible. Every moment is consumed with the anxiety of not measuring up, preventing you from participating in activities that once brought you happiness or peace. As time goes on, this ceaseless pressure begins to extract a heavy toll on both your mental and physical well-being. You find yourself grappling with persistent feelings of exhaustion, a constant state of fatigue that shadows your every effort. Alongside this, an undercurrent of bitterness starts to surface, stemming from the realization that the joy and fulfillment you desire seem perpetually out of reach, leaving you disillusioned and worn down by your own expectations.

Take the experience of Sarah, an eldest daughter who excelled academically and professionally, yet constantly felt stressed and anxious. Despite her numerous achievements, she never felt satisfied with her performance, always finding areas where she believed she fell short. This relentless self-scrutiny led to prolonged periods of burnout, causing her to resent the very responsibilities she once embraced with enthusiasm.

Another illustration is Maria, who secured a prestigious job and consistently delivered exceptional results. However, she struggled with imposter syndrome, believing that her success was due to external factors rather than her own capabilities. This belief prevented her from fully enjoying her achievements and caused her to incessantly strive for validation, both at work and at home. Her relentless pursuit of perfection left her physically drained and emotionally spent, impacting her overall quality of life.

Balancing Pleasing Yourself With Pleasing Others

Fear of judgment also plays a crucial role in shaping how eldest daughters interact with others. Growing up under scrutinizing eyes, you begin to internalize the need for approval, which can then extend into your professional and social lives. You may avoid sharing ideas or taking risks, worried about potential criticism. This hesitancy stifles creativity and innovation, restricting your potential to grow and thrive in various environments.

Imposter syndrome exacerbates these fears, causing you to devalue your contributions. You might constantly second-guess your abilities, seeking reassurance from others instead of trusting your judgment. This reliance on external validation creates a feedback loop where you perpetually aim to prove yourself, further amplifying your stress and anxiety.

On a lighter note, the desire to excel can foster remarkable resilience and perseverance. Many eldest daughters develop strong problem-solving skills and a commendable work ethic. However, these strengths often come at the cost of personal well-being. The challenge lies in balancing the drive for excellence with self-compassion and recognizing that imperfection is not synonymous with failure.

Navigating the balance between meeting expectations and prioritizing personal happiness is a complex and often challenging task. It requires a significant shift in mindset where individuals learn to set realistic goals that align with their true values and aspirations. This process involves appreciating one's efforts and achievements, recognizing that progress is a journey rather than a destination, and steering clear of the all-too-common trap of perfectionism.

By embracing imperfections and viewing them as opportunities for growth, individuals can foster resilience and adaptability in the face of difficulties. Additionally, understanding that setbacks and failures do not define one's worth or capabilities is crucial for cultivating self-compassion. These essential steps not only help in reducing stress but also contribute to the development of a healthier, more fulfilling life that values personal well-being over societal pressures.

The Unpaid Emotional Labor

Eldest daughters often find themselves in the unenviable position of being the emotional backbone of their families. They provide consistent emotional support to parents and siblings—an act that, while commendable, can lead to considerable emotional fatigue. This exhaustion arises because they frequently prioritize the emotional needs of others over their own, compromising their well-being.

For instance, in your family, you may be the confidant for each member, helping them resolve personal issues, offering a listening ear, and smoothing over conflicts. This role, although critical for family harmony, can sometimes leave you feeling emotionally drained. You are expected to be perpetually available for everyone, which often forces you to neglect your needs and desires in the process. Over time, this self-sacrificing behavior can lead to anxiety, depression, or chronic stress.

You may also have a tendency to internalize the stresses and conflicts within your family. Whenever there is tension, for example, you might assume that it's partly your fault and that you need to do something to bring peace. Or when one of your younger siblings is acting out, you might feel partly to blame for not being a good role model that they can look up to. As a result of internalizing family stress and conflict, you take on everyone's problems and may not have an immediate outlet to release them.

Absorbing all of this stress can have long-lasting psychological effects, such as developing a sense of inadequacy, codependency, or being a people-pleaser. Recognizing when you are emotionally overstretched and taking a step back is the first step to regaining mental and emotional balance.

Waiting for the Next Family Feud

The constant preparation for anticipated family crises is a pervasive aspect of life for many eldest daughters. You may often function as the family's emergency responder, staying vigilant and preparing to step in whenever a crisis arises.

While this readiness can cultivate strong problem-solving skills, it also places an enormous burden on your mental health. The unending cycle of anticipating and managing crises denies you the opportunity for self-reflection and healing. In the end, your life becomes consumed with caretaking duties, leaving little room for personal growth or for the pursuit of passions and interests outside your family obligations.

Your role as the emotional support provider, stress absorber, and crisis manager is demanding and often unrecognized. You may even carry these burdens silently, to avoid potential backlash or the stoking of family tensions. Your family members may have not developed the emotional range and intelligence to have open and constructive conversations about these invisible expectations you are carrying. Thus, you choose to spare yourself another conflict and continue to suffer alone.

It's crucial to understand that without establishing emotional boundaries, your family members will likely keep making requests of you without considering how their needs might be stifling your own. This situation can lead to feelings of resentment and overwhelm, as you continuously prioritize their demands over your own well-being.

In addition to this, the belief that your family members cannot solve problems on their own could be the reason why you come to their rescue all the time, preventing them from learning crucial life skills and developing their own problem-solving abilities. By failing to set these necessary boundaries, you may inadvertently hinder their growth while also neglecting your own emotional needs. Recognizing this dynamic is the first step toward building healthier relationships built on mutual respect and understanding.

It's important to start seeing your family members as capable human beings with great potential to become the heroes of their own stories. The emotional labor you provide for them is something they can learn to source from within. Every now and again, when you have the time and emotional capacity to assist, you can definitely do so. However, for everyday issues, trust each family member to apply their minds to solving their own crises.

You need to learn to set boundaries and advocate for your needs without guilt, and the tools and strategies offered in this book are a great place to start. However, in the long term, seeking external support, whether from friends, support groups, or mental health professionals, can provide much-needed relief and validation. As society becomes more aware of the unique challenges faced by eldest daughters, there is hope for greater appreciation and support for your invaluable contributions to family dynamics.

The Eldest Daughter Survival Kit

Every eldest daughter knows that the role comes with its own set of challenges, but what if you had a survival kit to help you navigate it all? Think of this as your go-to guide for handling the unique situations you face with humor, grace, and a dash of magic. *The Eldest Daughter Survival Kit* is filled with metaphorical items designed to empower you and make you smile—even when it feels like the weight of the world is on your shoulders. So, let's dive into the essentials every eldest daughter should have in her kit!

The Superhero Cape

Every eldest daughter needs a metaphorical cape to remind her of her inner strength and resilience. This cape symbolizes her ability to swoop in and save the day when family crises arise, but it's also a reminder that she can take it off when she needs a break.

Wear your invisible cape proudly when you're stepping up to solve problems, but don't forget: Sometimes, it's okay to hang up the cape and let someone else take charge.

Earplugs of Serenity

These magical earplugs filter out all the noise of unrealistic demands and unsolicited advice from family members. They help you focus on what truly matters—your own voice and needs.

Pop them in when you're feeling overwhelmed by family expectations or when you need to tune out guilt trips and focus on your well-being.

The Boundary-Setting Magic Wand

This wand gives you the power to create healthy boundaries with a flick of your wrist. It's enchanted to help you say "no" with confidence and kindness, and without the usual guilt.

Wave this wand when you're asked to take on too much or when you need to protect your time and energy. It's especially handy for deflecting last-minute requests or unnecessary obligations.

The Infinite Patience Potion

A little drop of this potion goes a long way! It's a metaphorical elixir that boosts your patience levels to superhuman heights—perfect for dealing with repetitive questions, sibling squabbles, or those times when everyone seems to need you all at once.

Sip this potion (figuratively, of course) whenever you feel your patience wearing thin. It's your secret weapon for staying calm and collected under pressure, but remember: Patience is not infinite, and it's okay to say "enough is enough."

The Self-Care Compass

This compass always points to what you need most at any given moment—whether it's rest, fun, or a little "me time." It's a reminder that self-care isn't selfish; you must put your needs first to continue being the amazing eldest daughter you are.

Follow the direction of your self-care compass when you're feeling lost amid the sea of responsibilities. Whether it's guiding you toward a quiet afternoon with a book or an evening out with friends, this compass will lead you back to yourself.

The Eldest Daughter Survival Kit isn't just a collection of whimsical items—it's a reminder that you have everything you need to navigate your role with confidence, humor, and love. Each "item" symbolizes the tools and strengths you already possess, along with the permission to take care of yourself as you take care of others. So, the next time you're feeling the weight of being the eldest daughter, reach into your kit and remember: You've got this!

Concluding Thoughts

This chapter has uncovered the intricate pressures and responsibilities faced by eldest daughters, revealing how these expectations create an invisible burden that shapes their emotional well-being and life choices. By exploring the roles of mediator, caretaker, and emotional support provider, we see how eldest daughters often sacrifice their needs for family harmony, leading to chronic dissatisfaction and self-neglect.

Understanding these dynamics highlights the necessity of recognizing and balancing family roles to prevent burnout and emotional distress. In the next chapter, we explore how cultural norms, gender roles, and media representations shape the experiences of eldest daughters, often reinforcing the pressures they face.

"The most common way people give up their power is by thinking they don't have any."

Alice Walker

Chapter 3

Culture, Trends, and On-Screen Sisters

Being the "Big Sis" in Different Cultures

Eldest daughters from different cultural backgrounds are raised in environments that set specific expectations for them. These expectations, whether coming from their parents or communities, shape their identities and roles within their families. By understanding the diverse cultural influences at play, we can appreciate the unique challenges and strengths these resilient women bring to their households and communities.

Asian Culture

In many Asian cultures, eldest daughters are seen as emotional caretakers, with a strong emphasis on family loyalty and support. In particular, South Asian families praise female submission and obedience as virtues, and one of the duties of parents is to teach their daughters, especially the eldest, how to serve others and play a supportive role (Shahid, 2023). Some of the tasks they can be expected to manage at home include doing household chores, caring for younger siblings, and providing emotional support to their parents.

Of course, not every Asian family follows these practices. In most cases, the eldest daughters are relied upon heavily in lower income families or families where parents are occupied with work. Their caregiving roles become crucial, enhancing the family's overall well-being. The societal pressure to excel felt by Asian eldest daughters in these roles can lead to significant personal sacrifices as they strive to meet the high standards set by their families and culture.

Western/European Culture

In contrast, Western or European perspectives on eldest daughters often emphasize leadership and independence. These eldest daughters are frequently encouraged to be self-sufficient and empowered.

Thanks to the influence of feminism, many eldest daughters are raised to choose their own paths instead of being assigned a path by their parents. Yet, while this does help to ease the burden of being the eldest child, it doesn't completely remove the pressure that eldest daughters feel to aim for perfection. Their empowerment comes with potential burdens, such as the desire to prove themselves as being capable of leaders and nurturers by juggling academic, professional, and household duties.

In the long run, they may struggle to balance their desire for autonomy with their ingrained caregiving instincts.

African Culture

African cultures also place significant demands on eldest daughters, who often take on a lot of emotional and physical responsibilities within their households. From a young age, these daughters are tasked with supporting their parents in various capacities. At the expense of their caregiving roles, they miss out on opportunities to further their education, seek employment, and become fully independent.

In low-income households, eldest daughters may be expected to start working from a young age, not for their own enrichment but to help with financial responsibilities and the needs of their younger siblings.

On the one hand, this dynamic enables African eldest daughters to develop strong leadership skills and a deep sense of empathy, but on the other, it can lead to feelings of being overwhelmed and undervalued.

Middle Eastern/Islamic Culture

In Middle Eastern Islamic families, the role of the eldest daughter is often associated with maintaining family cohesion and contributing to socioeconomic stability. These daughters are expected to uphold family honor and ensure the smooth functioning of the household. They frequently assist with household management, support their siblings' education, and contribute to the family's financial well-being.

The societal expectations placed on eldest daughters in Middle Eastern cultures are influenced by collectivist values that prioritize family unity and interdependence (Abudi, 2011). While these responsibilities can instill a strong sense of duty and accomplishment, they can also impose significant pressure and limit personal freedom.

The diverse expectations and roles assigned to eldest daughters across different cultures highlight the impact of cultural norms in influencing our life outcomes. In each context, these daughters navigate a unique set of challenges and opportunities, shaping their life experiences and perspectives in profound ways.

Understanding these cultural nuances allows you to reflect on how your family demands are influenced by your upbringing and what you believe your role is within your family and in the broader society. When you were a child, you may not have questioned why certain tasks were assigned to you and not to other siblings at home because those practices were normalized. However, now that you are older, you might look back at your past and find some obligations unfair, or even abusive.

Your Place in the Family Matters

In traditional families, eldest daughters experience the unspoken pressure to live up to their mothers' nurturing expectations. This is because society often sees them as being surrogate mother figures. As such, it's common for eldest daughters to learn domestic skills like cooking, cleaning, and nursing children at a young age. Unconsciously, they are imitating their mothers and cultivating skills which they believe will be valuable in life.

Nevertheless, not all eldest daughters manage to live up to the example set by their mothers. For instance, they may not be great cooks or may not manage to juggle multiple tasks. When they struggle to meet these standards, they may experience intense feelings of failure, guilt, and incompetence.

Depending on how traditional their community is, some may even judge these women for not displaying traditional feminine qualities. For instance, an eldest daughter who excels in school might still feel inadequate if she perceives that her academic success comes at the expense of her ability to care for her younger siblings or assist in household management.

Societal norms and cultural traditions also play a pivotal role in perpetuating gender-based expectations. For instance, cultural attitudes often suggest that young girls rather than young boys should prioritize family obligations over personal aspirations. In many societies, young girls are groomed from an early age to become homemakers, since this is the role they are assumed to play when they grow up. This societal pressure amplifies the burden on the eldest daughters, who feel compelled to follow this life path even at the expense of their own goals.

Being raised in such an environment can lead to eldest daughters feeling a heavy weight of guilt when choosing career fields or interests that deviate from their traditional expectations. Deep down, they may feel like they owe something to their family members and that they cannot be "selfish" enough to pursue their unconventional dreams. Many eldest daughters have abandoned their goals for the sake of investing their resources into caring for and assisting their family members.

So, what about the middle or youngest daughters? Do they feel the same pressures to choose family obligations over aspirations? While some may resonate with this experience, many middle or youngest daughters will not be expected to take on leadership roles. This means that they have more freedom to decide how involved they want to be in the family affairs. For example, if an opportunity to study abroad was presented to three sisters, the eldest would be less likely to accept the offer since she feels responsible for looking after her parents. The middle and youngest sisters would consider the offer and possibly take it.

The same applies to getting married. It's not uncommon for younger siblings (male or female) to get married first. Unlike the eldest siblings, they have fewer family responsibilities (both monetary and nonmonetary) that they need to take care of or settle before they decide to get hitched. And when the eldest siblings do eventually get married, the burden of family responsibilities does not end. They typically find a way to merge their two lives and juggle the duties of their new and biological families.

Sibling rivalry between the eldest and younger daughters is, to some extent, fueled by these unequal expectations. The eldest daughter feels that her younger sibling is entitled and out of touch with reality, while the younger sibling doesn't understand where their eldest sibling's rage comes from. They may both be women, raised in the same traditional background; however, their life outcomes won't look the same. As an eldest daughter, watching your younger sister live carefree, jumping from one pursuit to another, can be emotionally triggering because you believe that you cannot do the same without feeling guilt or shame.

Media Myths and Misses About Eldest Daughters

Media often falls back on stereotypes that paint eldest daughters as overly submissive or burdened by obligation. For example, they may be the overly involved sister who is called by family members to bail them out of jail or defend them in the principal's office. They may also be the sibling who sacrifices their career ambitions to take care of their aging parents. These characterizations reinforce limiting beliefs that the eldest daughter's worth revolves around their family contributions.

Additionally, these types of depictions can cause viewers to undermine the role and impact of eldest daughters on family life. When they are shown as constantly sacrificing their own needs for the sake of others without recognition or reward, it can make their duties seem trivial or less important instead of them being duties that should be associated with a sense of accomplishment. The weight of these negative portrayals can undermine their sense of self-worth and erode their confidence, making it harder for them to assert themselves both at home and in their professional lives.

Social media trends add another layer to this dynamic, offering both opportunities and challenges for eldest daughters. Platforms like Instagram and TikTok have become spaces where eldest daughters share their experiences, creating a sense of community and dialogue around shared struggles. Hashtags like #eldestdaughterproblems and #oldersiblinglife have brought visibility to their unique challenges, normalizing conversations about mental health, pressure, and family roles.

This normalization can be validating, helping eldest daughters realize that they are not alone in their experiences. It can create solidarity and even lead to collective empowerment. However, the nature of social media also amplifies the pressure of public comparison. Scrolling through curated images and stories of seemingly perfect lives can exacerbate feelings of inadequacy.

Eldest daughters might find themselves comparing their behind-the-scenes struggles with the highlight reels of others. This constant comparison can be mentally and emotionally draining, reinforcing insecurities and heightening anxiety. Additionally, the performative aspect of social media means that some users might downplay their difficulties to appear more appealing or accomplished, creating a skewed representation of reality.

Take a moment to think about how the media has impacted your emotional well-being. Consider the shows or movies that you frequently watch. How do they portray eldest daughters? Do the female characters live empowered lives or reinforce stereotypes? Shifting to social media, in what ways does being on social networking platforms validate your eldest-daughter experiences? On the other hand, how do these platforms create increasing pressure to be more and do more?

Since the media can sometimes inflate real-life situations, it's important to consciously choose what content you consume. Entertainment factor aside, some eldest daughter archetypes are outdated and harmful to your self-concept. The same can be said about social media. Some pages or influencers on social media may portray an eldest daughter lifestyle with unrealistic standards, tricking you into believing that you actually can do it all and that if you don't, there is something wrong with you. Ultimately, your job is to discern between the type of content and social messages that are realistic and the type that is just for clickbait.

Empowering Lessons From Eldest Daughters in Pop Culture

Being the eldest daughter is a bit like stepping into a role that's been prewritten for you, complete with expectations, responsibilities, and a dash of sibling rivalry. But what if you decide to flip the script? In pop culture, we see many eldest daughters who have done just that—defying traditional roles, carving their own paths, and inspiring us along the way. These characters remind us that being the eldest daughter isn't just about responsibility; it's also about strength, creativity, and the power to rewrite your own story.

Let's take a look at five iconic eldest daughters in movies, TV shows, and books who broke the mold and lived empowered lives, all while keeping their sense of humor intact.

Elizabeth Bennet From Pride and Prejudice

Elizabeth Bennet, the sharp-witted eldest daughter of the Bennet family, is a shining example of someone who refuses to let societal expectations define her. In a time when marriage was considered the ultimate goal for women, Lizzy stood out by prioritizing her happiness, intellect, and independence. She's not afraid to speak her mind, challenge authority, or reject a proposal (even if it's from a wealthy suitor like Mr. Collins). Her determination to marry for love rather than convenience was groundbreaking for that period, making her a role model for eldest daughters everywhere.

Empowering Lesson: Don't be afraid to stand up for what you believe in, even if it goes against the norm. Your happiness and values should come first.

Lisa Simpson From The Simpsons

Lisa Simpson, the overachieving eldest daughter of the Simpson family, is a character who consistently breaks the mold. Despite being just eight years old, Lisa's intelligence, moral compass, and passion for social justice set her apart. She's not afraid to challenge authority, question the status quo, or take a stand on issues she cares about—even if it makes her unpopular. Lisa's love for learning and her unwavering commitment to doing the right thing make her a powerful example of how eldest daughters can use their influence for good.

Empowering Lesson: Intelligence and integrity are your greatest strengths. Use them to make a difference, no matter how young—or old—you are.

Jo March From Little Women

Jo, the second eldest sister in *Little Women*, carries the weight of her family's financial struggles while fiercely pursuing her dreams of becoming a writer. She defies traditional gender norms with her boyish character and refusal to live up to the fashion and social standards for women in New England during the Civil War. Jo challenges societal norms, constantly pushing for her own success while also ensuring the well-being of her family. While her sometimes inappropriate outspokenness doesn't make her appealing to some, it shows her humanity and authenticity.

Empowering Lesson: Pursue your passions and ambitions fearlessly, even when others question your motives or make you feel like an outsider.

Katara From Avatar: The Last Airbender

Katara, the eldest daughter of the Southern Water Tribe, takes on the role of caretaker and leader after the loss of her mother. Despite the immense responsibilities on her young shoulders, Katara never loses sight of her dreams and goals. She becomes a master Waterbender, fights for justice, and leads with compassion. Katara's journey is one of growth, resilience, and empowerment as she learns to balance her responsibilities with her own desires and aspirations.

Empowering Lesson: You can be both a leader and a dreamer. Don't let your responsibilities hold you back from pursuing your own goals.

Sansa Stark From Game of Thrones

Sansa Stark, the eldest daughter of House Stark, starts her journey as a naive young girl with dreams of becoming a queen. But as she faces betrayal, loss, and hardship, Sansa grows into a strong, cunning, and resilient leader. She learns to navigate the dangerous political landscape of Westeros, ultimately emerging as a powerful ruler in her own right. Sansa's transformation from a sheltered girl to a wise and determined leader is a testament to the strength and resilience that many eldest daughters possess.

Empowering Lesson: Life's challenges can shape you into a stronger, wiser person. Embrace your growth, and don't be afraid to take your place as a leader.

These pop culture icons remind us that being the eldest daughter is about more than just meeting expectations—it's about exceeding them in your own unique way. Whether it's through intelligence, bravery, compassion, or resilience, these characters show us that the eldest daughter's role is one of power and potential. So, take a page from their books (or scripts) and remember that you have the strength to define your own story. After all, you're the heroine of your own life, and the best is yet to come.

Concluding Thoughts

This chapter has investigated the myriad ways in which cultural norms, gender roles, and media representations shape the lives of eldest daughters. Whether acting as caregivers in Asian families, leaders in Western contexts, or stabilizing forces in African and Middle Eastern households, eldest daughters navigate a complex web of expectations that impact their sense of self and their life choices. These experiences reveal both the strengths they possess and the pressures they endure, highlighting the resilience required to meet such high demands.

In the next chapter, we look at the importance of reclaiming individuality and self-worth in the face of external pressures.

"I can't think of any better representation of beauty than someone who is unafraid to be herself."

Emma Stone

Chapter 4
Reclaim Your Identity and Self-Worth

External Validation vs. Self-Acceptance

Reclaiming your individuality and self-worth can feel like an uphill battle, especially when external pressures constantly push you to conform. The weight of these pressures and the quest for validation can overshadow personal growth and lead to a sense of inadequacy and burnout. Think about all of the times you abandoned your needs because you felt like the right thing to do was respond to a family need. In those confusing moments, you were training yourself to derive a sense of self-worth through the things you do for others instead of who you are as an individual.

The internal conflict between "doing" and "being" is probably one that you have lived through for many years. On the one hand, your inner critic tells you that unless you step up your game and prove to your loved ones that they can trust and rely on you, you are not playing your role as an elder daughter. However, there is also another part of you that rejects this idea of perpetual self-sacrifice and desires to simply be authentic and present in the moment, living a life that is grounded in your values and purpose.

Focusing too heavily on "doing" rather than "being" can detract you from pursuing personal goals. Your decisions may be driven by the fear of disappointing family instead of exploring your personal interests, genuine passions, and ambitions. Moreover, you might choose a career path that aligns with your family's expectations rather than one that truly excites you. This divergence not only affects professional satisfaction but also hampers your long-term fulfillment and happiness.

To break free from this cycle, it is essential to recognize the difference between getting constructive feedback and exhibiting unhealthy, approval-seeking behavior. Constructive feedback aims to improve your skills and performance while approval-seeking behavior tends to prioritize pleasing others at one's own expense. Another difference is that constructive feedback scrutinizes your actions, not who you are as a person. This type of feedback allows you to reflect on what you could improve about your approach to situations; it doesn't seek to destabilize your sense of self by raising questions about your competence.

By understanding this distinction, you can start to recognize whenever your thoughts are helpful or harmful, or whenever comments made by others seek to bring out the best or worst in you. For example, your inner critic is infamous for giving negative feedback that magnifies your shortcomings while undermining your strengths. Would your critical thoughts be considered constructive? No, they wouldn't. Instead, they would fuel attention-seeking behavior as an attempt to prove your worthiness to others.

Recognizing the difference between constructive feedback and attention-seeking behaviors also enables you to encourage people to be free to express what they think or feel in a manner that doesn't invalidate your own thoughts and feelings. In other words, you expect others to acknowledge that, just like them, you are a human being who makes mistakes, experiences mood swings, and won't always make the best decisions.

Embrace Who You Are, Unapologetically

Building a foundation of self-worth is an important journey that you will find yourself on when seeking to address and heal from EDS. Self-acceptance is the key to making this journey impactful. Embracing practices that encourage self-acceptance helps you develop a healthier relationship with yourself. It can also allow you to recognize your strengths and weaknesses without judgment.

Cultivating self-acceptance involves carrying out the following strategies that can be integrated into your daily life.

Practice Self-Reflection

Take time to reflect on your personal experiences, feelings, and reactions to understand yourself better and uncover the underlying "why" behind everything you do. For example, you might reflect on why you say "yes" to people when you want to say "no," or why you struggle to follow through on plans that involve practicing self-care.

Be careful not to judge yourself or allow the inner critic to take over the exercise. Self-reflection is not about defending your thoughts, feelings, and behaviors, but instead about getting a deeper understanding of the patterns you reinforce. Keeping a journal can be particularly beneficial, as it provides a private space to explore your thoughts and emotions without judgment. Through consistent self-reflection, you can identify patterns of behavior driven by the need for validation and work toward altering them.

Identify Influential Voices

Mapping out influences from family and peers helps you identify whose beliefs, opinions, and expectations hold a significant influence on your behaviors. The earliest influence often comes from your parents, whose attitudes and behaviors shaped your childhood perceptions of self-worth. Understanding these dynamics allows for greater awareness of problematic patterns of behaviors and how to address them.

Create a visual map of important relationships and note how each key person in your life (or from your past) influences your feelings and decisions. This exercise can highlight both positive and negative influences. For instance, if a parent's approval significantly impacts your self-esteem, acknowledging this influence can help you mitigate its effects. You can also reflect on whether the influential voices in your life are supportive or detrimental to your health.

Connect With Supportive Communities

Surrounding yourself with understanding peers is affirming and reveals the amazing woman you are, reducing your reliance on negative influences. Imagine being around people who share similar perspectives as you, who embrace your quirkiness, and who show compassion toward you whenever you aren't feeling your best. Shared experiences within these communities can challenge the disempowering narrative of needing family approval to feel good about yourself.

Engaging in groups or forums where eldest daughters share their stories and support each other can be empowering. These communities create a safe space to express struggles and triumphs, reinforcing the idea that seeking self-acceptance is a collective journey rather than an isolated endeavor.

Overcoming the Imposter

Imposter syndrome is a psychological phenomenon where individuals doubt their accomplishments and fear being exposed as a "fraud." It manifests in various ways, including persistent self-doubt, attributing success to luck and an irrational fear of failure.

As an eldest daughter, these feelings may be amplified by the responsibilities you shouldered from a young age, such as caregiving for younger siblings or meeting the high academic standards set by your parents. Acknowledging that imposter syndrome is a common experience can help you begin to dismantle the belief that you are alone or inherently flawed.

To combat imposter syndrome, practical coping strategies are essential. These strategies can help you alter your mindset and develop a more positive self-image.

Reframe Negative Thoughts

Instead of focusing on perceived failures or shortcomings, you can train yourself to recognize your strengths and successes. This shift in perspective transforms self-criticism into self-compassion. For example, when faced with a challenging task, instead of thinking, "I'm not good enough," you might reframe it to, "I have the skills and experience to tackle this."

Reframing negative thoughts teaches you to question your beliefs before assuming they are true. Not every thought that you think about is helpful or constructive. Some thoughts could be based on fear or triggered by unresolved emotional issues or relationships from the past. Being less reactive to your thoughts gives you a moment to pause and scrutinize them, thereby separating facts from fiction.

Find a Mentor

Mentorship plays a pivotal role in overcoming feelings of inadequacy. Having a mentor who is also an eldest daughter and can share other similarities with you provides guidance and support, offering you a fresh perspective on situations that may seem overwhelming. Your mentor can share their own experiences with imposter syndrome so that you can realize that these feelings are not unique to you. By learning from what they have been through, you can be assured that you are not alone and can overcome imposter syndrome too.

Mentorship can also offer valuable lessons in setting boundaries and prioritizing self-care. By observing how your mentors manage similar responsibilities and challenges, you gain practical tools for managing your own life. A mentor can encourage you to take necessary breaks, pursue personal interests, and develop a healthy balance between caregiving duties and self-care. Over time, you can learn to value your well-being and growth as much as your role within the family.

Establish Personal Milestones

To address the tendency of downplaying your accomplishments, often a symptom of imposter syndrome, you can create personalized milestones to recognize your achievements and sustain momentum. These milestones serve as markers of progress that validate the sacrifices you have made along your personal growth journey. Personalized milestones can range from small daily goals to long-term aspirations, encompassing both professional and personal development. For example, one of your milestones could be making Sundays your rest days where you focus on relaxing or catching up on sleep.

To establish meaningful milestones, reflect on your values and passions. Ask yourself questions like, "What aspects of my life bring genuine fulfillment? What skills or knowledge do I wish to acquire?" By aligning your milestones with personal values, they become more than just check marks on a list—they become integral parts of your journey toward self-fulfillment and self-worth.

Recognizing Self-Worth: Building Internal Validation

Reflecting on childhood experiences causes you to recognize moments where your worth was measured by how well you met family expectations. Carrying over this belief into your adulthood has made you think that your self-worth was conditional, even though this isn't true.

You can shift this perspective by understanding that your self-worth is inherent and immutable. The value that you are born with has nothing to do with the skills or accomplishments you have acquired. Teaching yourself to see value for who you are, not what you can do, gives you the freedom to live authentically and without the fear of external judgment.

Self-awareness plays a vital role in recognizing your self-worth and identifying the limiting beliefs that are getting in the way of truly appreciating yourself. You can scrutinize your beliefs, assessing where they come from and what type of message they bring across about you. For instance, are they influenced by your family's opinions or societal standards? Recognizing these influences can help begin the process of redefining self-worth on your terms.

Here are more ways to start seeking worth from within rather than from your surroundings.

Being Aware of Your Thoughts and Feelings

Mindfulness is the powerful practice of anchoring your mind in the present moment so that you can fully engage with the thoughts, feelings, sensations, and external activities around you without judgment. By practicing mindfulness, you can tune into your inner self and affirm your feelings and worth without needing external validation.

Research has shown that practicing mindfulness regularly can lead to positive brain changes such as increased gray matter density in the regions associated with empathy, emotional regulation, and decision-making (Kuo et al., 2022). This suggests that regular mindfulness meditation can enhance your ability to regulate emotions, which is crucial in developing self-validation.

One effective mindfulness technique is mindful breathing. It starts with you setting aside time each day to focus your breathing. It could be during your five-minute coffee break at work or before you go to bed. Notice the air flowing into your nose and out through your mouth. Take deep breaths that travel to your belly to ensure that you are filling your lungs; this also makes the exhale feel satisfying. If your mind wanders during this practice, gently shift your attention back to your breathing. In the end, you should feel grounded in the present moment.

Another beneficial practice is mindful journaling, where you write down your thoughts and experiences without filtering them. This allows you to observe your feelings and validate them internally. For example, if you feel overwhelmed by responsibilities, writing about these emotions can help you acknowledge and accept them, reinforcing your self-worth.

Creating a Personal Value System

Establishing a personal value system is essential in recognizing your self-worth based on your beliefs rather than family expectations. A personal value system reflects the principles and standards that are truly important to you and that guide your behavior and decisions.

To create a personal value system, start by identifying your core values. These might include honesty, compassion, creativity, or independence. Remind yourself of past experiences where you felt proud of who you are. What qualities were you exhibiting in those moments? Those qualities likely align with your core values.

After identifying your core values, find practical ways of incorporating them into your everyday life. For example, you can make decisions that honor these values, even if they go against family expectations. If independence is a core value, prioritize actions that promote your autonomy, such as pursuing a career you're passionate about, even if it doesn't align with your family's wishes.

Celebrating Individual Achievements

Regularly acknowledging and celebrating your achievements counters any lingering feelings of inadequacy that may stem from a lifetime of high expectations and criticisms. It starts by creating a habit of recognizing your progress or the things that you naturally do well, no matter how small they may seem to you. Maintain a journal where you document things you're proud of each day. This could be anything from completing a challenging task at work to taking time for yourself despite a busy schedule. Writing these achievements reinforces your recognition of your effort and worth.

Additionally, celebrate these achievements in meaningful ways. Treat yourself to something special, share your success with close friends, or simply take a moment to reflect on your hard work and dedication. Celebrations don't need to be grand; the key is to create positive reinforcement for your efforts. In situations where external pressures are overwhelming, remind yourself of your past successes to build self-confidence and a sense of self-efficacy.

Reflecting on what you've achieved in your life can provide the motivation you need to affirm your inherent worth.

Eldest Daughter Affirmations: Pep Talks for the Everyday Hero

Being the eldest daughter is often like being an unsung superhero—juggling responsibilities, managing crises, and always being there for everyone. But even superheroes need encouragement, regular reminders to take care of themselves, and a little humor to get through the day.

These affirmations are designed to uplift, empower, and inject a bit of light-heartedness into your often weighty role of the eldest daughter. Use them whenever you need a boost, a smile, or just a reminder that you're doing an incredible job.

Affirmations

1. My identity extends beyond the roles I play for others. I have passions, talents, and aspirations that deserve to be nurtured.

2. Just like every superhero has a fortress of solitude, I have the right to my own time and space to recharge, guilt-free.

3. Self-care is not a luxury; it's essential. When I prioritize my well-being, I'm better equipped to support those I love.

4. Boundaries are a sign of self-respect. It's okay if they're met with resistance; they are necessary for my peace and happiness.

5. I don't need to be perfect to be valuable. My efforts, even when imperfect, are worthy of recognition and pride.

6. My worth isn't tied to my achievements or to how much I help others. I am worthy of love and celebration just for being me.

7. I don't have to carry everything on my own. Asking for support is a sign of strength, not weakness.

8. It's not my job to fix everything for everyone. My happiness matters, and I have the right to pursue it without guilt.

9. I'm not bound by expectations or traditions. I can forge my own journey, one that reflects who I truly am and what I want out of life.

10. My influence goes beyond tasks and responsibilities. By being true to myself, I inspire others to do the same.

These affirmations are your personal pep talks—reminders that you are strong, capable, and deserving of all the love and care you give to others. Keep them close, repeat them often, and know that you are more than enough just as you are.

Concluding Thoughts

In this chapter, we discussed how seeking approval from others can lead to a cycle of dependency and burnout, making it challenging to pursue one's genuine passions.

Understanding the difference between constructive feedback and unhealthy approval-seeking is key to breaking free from this pattern, allowing for choices that align with inner values. Additionally, recognizing the influences from family dynamics and connecting with supportive communities can provide affirmation and reduce isolation. By asserting themselves and being around understanding peers, eldest daughters can shift their focus from external validation to internal growth.

In the next chapter, we focus on how eldest daughters can effectively manage relationships and establish healthy boundaries in various aspects of their lives.

"The woman who doesn't require validation from anyone is the most feared individual on the planet."

Mohadesa Najumi

Chapter 5
Navigating Relationships and Boundaries

Sibling Relationships and the Potential for Favoritism

Navigating the dynamics between yourself and your siblings can be a challenging task layered with responsibility and emotional complexity. The potential presence of favoritism in your family combined with the burden of caretaking is pivotal in shaping your sibling relationships, often placing you in an unfavorable position.

The primary issue at play is that you are expected by your parents to set a standard for your younger siblings. This expectation can have its privileges, such as being seen as a role model, but on the flip side, it can foster an environment ripe for resentment and conflict. When your parents—either intentionally or unintentionally—impose high standards for you to meet, it creates a division within the family. There are certain behaviors that would be seen as inappropriate for you but acceptable for your younger siblings, since you are the eldest and must set the precedent for them. Meanwhile, younger siblings might perceive themselves as living in your shadow, which can breed jealousy and result in strained relationships.

A key strategy for managing these pressures is recognizing personal limits. As the eldest daughter, you should understand your limitations and not overextend yourself to exceed them. Saying things like "I would love to help, but this weekend, I'm unavailable" establishes a boundary around how much of your time, efforts, and energy you can offer to others. Furthermore, it can improve your family relationships by managing their expectations of you.

Communicate with your family about what you can realistically handle. Practice sharing your thoughts, emotions, or concerns as they are, without embellishments. Understandably, it can be hard to be honest about your experiences, especially when your family is accustomed to seeing you juggle multiple duties and not show signs of being overwhelmed. You may feel guilt about exposing your vulnerabilities because, at the back of your mind, you desire to be an enviable role model who never disappoints your loved ones. However, consider the kind of example you are setting for your siblings when you hide your weaknesses and only show your strengths. Not only do they grow up with an unrealistic perception of personal growth (i.e., that some people don't fail at anything), but they can also internalize shame when they happen to experience failure, believing that something must be wrong with them since they never saw you fail and bounce back.

Labels such as "the responsible one" or "the problem-solver" can trap you in restrictive roles. To be seen as responsible all the time implies that you cannot take a backseat in family situations and allow for other members to step up and take responsibility. If the crises aren't handled by you, nothing gets achieved. You also might feel pigeonholed by the label, limiting your freedom of expression and growth.

Instead of being assigned labels, families should focus on recognizing each member's unique strengths and potential. There should also be a standard of behavior that all family members are held to. For example, all family members should account for their mistakes, help out around the house, donate toward family outings or financial goals, or be expected to come up with solutions for common family problems.

Creating a healthy environment where all siblings feel valued and supported is essential for mitigating the adverse effects of favoritism and the burdensome expectations placed on eldest daughters. Parents should ensure equitable distribution of attention and resources, treating each child's accomplishments and needs with equal importance.

Encouraging sibling collaboration rather than competition encourages teamwork and mutual respect. In addition, allowing children to develop their own identities and interests without undue pressure reduces the likelihood of resentment and rivalry.

Mastering Negotiations With Parents

Parents are a child's first love. They were assigned to you at birth to ensure your survival. Their job was to provide a nurturing environment where you can grow and feel safe exploring the world. However, in real life, parent–child relationships are not always this idealistic. The eldest son or daughter is a parent's first child and first attempt at parenting. A lot of mistakes are made with the eldest that are adjusted when raising the middle or youngest child. Therefore, how you perceive your parents and the type of bond you share is unique from your younger siblings.

For example, your parents may have projected their hopes and fears onto you, often seeing you as an extension of their own unmet dreams and anxieties. This may have led to a range of pressures imposed on you, from academic achievement to career choices and even personal behavior. Such projections created a heavy burden on you, causing you to feel obligated to fulfill your parents' unfulfilled ambitions while suppressing your own desires.

One way to navigate this complex dynamic is through self-awareness and emotional intelligence. You need to recognize when you are internalizing your parents' projections and find ways to separate these from your own aspirations. It starts by learning to identify the influence of your parent's beliefs, values, and opinions on your understanding of who you are.

For example, your parents may have valued a traditional lifestyle and held conservative beliefs. You may have integrated these ideas in the way you live, preferring tradition over modern living. But take a moment to truly think about what kind of lifestyle makes you content. Do you sincerely love tradition or is it just familiar? Are there aspects of modern living that you support or desire to explore?

While there isn't anything wrong about sharing similar interests and beliefs with your parents, it's important to always question the bigger "why" behind your assertions to test whether those ideas come from your heart or have been borrowed from someone else.

Asserting Needs Enhances Self-Worth

Gaining the confidence to express your individuality can help you communicate your needs without guilt or the need for others' approval. Individuality is the freedom to be yourself and express your thoughts and feelings. Many times, the middle and youngest siblings are encouraged to embrace their individuality, whereas the eldest sibling is advised to follow in their parents' footsteps.

As an adult, you can teach yourself to express your authentic self at home. It starts with learning how to state what you need or what you cannot accept. One practical method is to establish nonnegotiables that are firm and not open to compromise. For example, setting aside a specific time each day for personal activities can be a nonnegotiable boundary. When your parents or siblings call during this time of day, they won't be able to reach you.

Communicating this clearly to family members helps ensure they are respected. For instance, you could say, "After 5:30 p.m., I am unavailable for calls because I'm spending quality time with my partner." Follow through by putting your phone on silent at 5:30 p.m. to avoid any disturbances. Additionally, establishing consequences for boundary violations reinforces their importance. For instance, if your 5:30 p.m. rule is violated, taking a step back and reiterating the need for that limit demonstrates its significance.

Building Healthy Friendships

The eldest daughters are often the leaders at home and in their social lives. Those who are accustomed to being caregivers may find themselves naturally slipping into similar roles within their friendships. This happens unconsciously due to their maternal instincts.

Recognizing what healthy friendship dynamics look like is essential in cultivating mutual support. Healthy friendships are characterized by reciprocal care, kindness, and understanding. There's a balance between giving and receiving, which makes the relationship mutually satisfying for everyone.

One way to ensure balanced friendships is by emphasizing quality over quantity. For example, you might feel pressured to maintain numerous friendships as a means of proving your sociability or worth. However, this can often lead to superficial connections that don't offer genuine support in times of need. Prioritizing fewer but deeper relationships allows you to focus on meaningful interactions.

To create quality friendships, you can start by reflecting on your friendship values—the principles that govern how you treat your friends and how you would like to be treated. Understanding what you stand for helps in articulating your feelings clearly. For instance, if honesty is a core value for you, having a friend who frequently omits truths can become a source of tension. By clearly communicating this value to your friends, it becomes easier to address conflicts directly and constructively.

Learning more about your friendship values requires introspection, but once they are identified, they serve as a guide during boundary setting, negotiations, and disagreements, helping you navigate these situations with integrity.

Honest communication is another cornerstone for maintaining healthy friendships. Clear communication can clarify expectations and alleviate stress, making relationships more manageable. For instance, if you feel overwhelmed by your responsibilities and need some time alone, communicating this need openly prevents misunderstandings and potential resentment. Maintaining honesty about your emotional limits leads to a supportive environment where your friends don't just react but understand and respect your needs.

It's important to reinforce the necessity of reasonable expectations in your friendships. Having standards for your friendships is not about pushing people away but about ensuring that you build relationships that remain healthy and mutually beneficial. Expectations such as respecting each other's time, being allowed to say no, setting limits to the amount of emotional labor you do, and prioritizing self-care help you maintain your well-being while nurturing your friendships. Establishing these expectations early in friendships can mitigate the risk of burnout and ensure that both parties' needs are considered when making decisions.

Dating Without the Drama

The roles you play in your family can frequently extend into your romantic relationships where you might unconsciously assume the position of caretaker, mirroring the duties you've taken on within your family. Establishing and maintaining boundaries in these relationships is crucial to avoid falling into patterns of obligation and emotional caretaking.

Recognizing this pattern is the first step toward cultivating genuine relationships. When you prioritize your romantic partner's needs over your own, it doesn't have the same nurturing effect as in a family setting. Instead, it can become problematic in romantic relationships, leading to codependency and emotional exhaustion. Take a moment to reflect on your tendency to do this and how it impacts your ability to express your individuality and receive support when you need it.

Healthy communication in romance involves clearly defining one's boundaries around time and availability. Practice being intentional about how often you spend time with your partner and communicate openly about your need for personal space and downtime.

Identifying authentic needs within a romantic relationship allows you to notice when you start to do things out of a sense of duty rather than desire and pause. Ask yourself what pressure you may be under and where the pressure comes from. Doing things out of a sense of duty can lead to resentment and erode mutual respect, perpetuating the same family patterns. By regularly checking in with yourself and your partner about what you both genuinely need from the relationship, you can cultivate an environment of honesty and support.

For instance, if spending Sunday afternoons alone to unwind feels necessary, communicating this need candidly ensures that both of you can adjust expectations respectfully. This transparency builds trust and highlights the importance of valuing one's needs alongside those of their partner.

Breaking the Rules: When the Eldest Daughter Says "No"

As the eldest daughter, you've been the go-to person for organizing family events, mediating sibling disputes, and offering a listening ear to friends and romantic partners alike. But what happens when you decide to break the mold and say "no"? It's not about rebellion for the sake of it—it's about reclaiming your time, energy, and peace of mind.

In this section, we'll explore five scenarios where saying "no" can feel like a small but mighty act of self-liberation. And don't worry, we'll keep it lighthearted and empowering, because sometimes, the most freeing word in your vocabulary is simply "no."

Saying "No" to Family Requests

Scenario: Your parents expect you to host the next family gathering—again—because you're "so good at it."

Response: "This year, I'm passing the baton! It's time for someone else to shine in the hosting spotlight. I'll bring dessert and my best dance moves, but the hosting crown is up for grabs."

Saying "no" doesn't mean abandoning your family; it's about sharing the load. Celebrate the act of delegating as a win for everyone—

especially you! You're still part of the fun, just without the stress of planning.

Saying "No" to Friends

Scenario: A friend asks you to help them move on short notice, assuming you'll drop everything to assist.

Response: "I'd love to help, but I've got my superhero cape in the laundry this weekend. How about I treat you to dinner after the move instead?"

Saying "no" doesn't mean you're not a good friend—it means you value your time and energy. Make your "no" playful and offer an alternative that's still supportive, ensuring that your friendship remains strong without sacrificing your own plans.

Saying "No" to Romantic Partners

Scenario: Your partner suggests a weekend getaway that sounds fun, but you're already feeling stretched thin.

Response: "That sounds amazing, but I'm in need of some 'me time' to recharge my superpowers. Let's plan for next month when I'll be fully energized and ready to enjoy every moment."

Self-care isn't selfish—it's essential! By saying "no" now, you're ensuring that you can say "yes" wholeheartedly later, making it a win-win for both of you. You're prioritizing quality time over simply showing up.

Saying "No" to Sibling Favors

Scenario: Your sibling wants you to help them with a project they've procrastinated on, expecting you to pull an all-nighter with them.

Response: "I'm all for sibling bonding, but tonight, I'm booked with a date—me, myself, and I. Let's plan for a future project when we can tackle it together without the rush."

Saying "no" to last-minute stress doesn't make you less supportive—it makes you a protector of your well-being. Encourage better planning next time and enjoy your guilt-free evening.

Saying "No" to Extra Work Responsibilities

Scenario: Your boss hints that you should take on an extra project at work because "you're the most reliable."

Response: "I appreciate the vote of confidence, but I'm currently maxed out with my current projects. How about we revisit this once I've cleared my plate?"

Saying "no" at work isn't a sign of weakness—it's a sign of strong boundaries. By managing your workload wisely, you're ensuring that the tasks you do take on are done with the excellence you're known for without burning yourself out.

In each of these scenarios, saying "no" can be uplifting because you recognize that your time and energy are valuable and that you have every right to protect them. So, the next time you're faced with a request that doesn't align with your needs, remember that "no" is a complete sentence, and sometimes, it's the most empowering one you can say.

Concluding Thoughts

This chapter has probed into the complex relationships eldest daughters navigate with their siblings, parents, friends, and romantic partners, highlighting the heavy expectations placed upon them. We've discussed the emotional pressures of favoritism, the high standards imposed by parents that can lead to stress, the imbalances of giving and receiving in friendships, and the need to discuss expectations and set boundaries in romantic relationships.

Moving forward, practical strategies such as setting nonnegotiables, encouraging open dialogue, and seeking support can make a significant difference in ensuring relationships are reciprocal and fair. By prioritizing their own interests and well-being, eldest daughters can build stronger, more balanced relationships within their families and beyond.

In the next chapter, we emphasize the importance of addressing anxiety, burnout, guilt, and shame for personal empowerment and well-being.

"I have learned that as long as I hold fast to my beliefs and values and follow my own moral compass, then the only expectations I need to live up to are my own."

Michelle Obama

Chapter 6
The Emotional Roller Coaster of Being the Eldest Daughter

Are You Feeling Anxious?

In many families, the eldest daughter is seen as the anchor—the one who holds everything and everyone together. This perception can be both empowering and overwhelming, since the constant striving to meet high expectations can lead to anxiety.

Recognizing these anxiety triggers can help you understand that your anxiety is not a personal failing but a response to external pressures. This realization can be liberating, providing a new perspective for your experiences and emotions. However, awareness alone is not enough. Effective coping mechanisms are essential to manage and mitigate the effects of this anxiety in the long term.

Exploring Your Anxiety Triggers

Recognizing anxiety triggers can be an important step in managing your role as the eldest daughter. A trigger can be anything that takes you out of your normal resting state and heightens your stress levels. Your triggers might include conflicts with your siblings, worries about aging parents, challenges at work, or personal relationships that need attention.

Understanding the Root of Panic Attacks

Do panic attacks sometimes feel random? Often, they are not random at all, but rather a culmination of stress and unresolved emotions. These episodes can feel overwhelming, leading to physical symptoms like a racing heart or difficulty breathing. It can feel like you are losing control, which might heighten your anxiety even more.

Understanding that there might be many underlying issues at play helps in processing these experiences. For example, work problems might combine with family tension and personal struggles, creating a perfect storm for a panic attack. On the other hand, your panic attacks may stem from having difficulty sharing your feelings, saying "no" to others, or asking for help when you feel overwhelmed. This often means that you don't have healthy outlets to release stress and regain inner balance and harmony.

Make Your Well-Being a Priority

For the eldest daughter in a family, you may feel the need to meet every request or take on every obligation that comes your way. However, it is important to understand that saying no is not only acceptable but also necessary for your well-being. Making your well-being a priority helps you define what you can and cannot handle, allowing for a healthier relationship with yourself and your loved ones. Here are some tips to help you get started:

- **Assess your current commitments.** Take a detailed look at your daily activities and identify what truly matters to you. For example, if you find yourself frequently overwhelmed by family gatherings or events, you might decide that you can attend every other event instead of all of them. By doing this, you create space in your schedule for your own interests or some needed quiet time. A practical step is to make a list of obligations, then highlight those that are enjoyable versus those that feel like a burden. This clarity can help you make informed choices about where to allocate your time and energy.

- **Create a designated 'me time.'** Allocate specific hours of the day to focus solely on yourself. It could be as simple as setting aside the first hour of the morning for a relaxing routine that includes activities such as journaling, reading, or taking a walk. Additionally, you may choose to implement technology-free periods where you can disconnect from family group chats or social media. This dedicated time helps recharge your mental and emotional batteries, reducing the anxiety that arises from constant communication and obligations.

- **Step back from family conflict.** Family dynamics can be complex and often involve emotional exchanges that take a toll on your well-being. If a particular family member tends to engage in conflict or brings up past issues, you can choose to limit your interaction with them when they seem troubled. This doesn't mean cutting ties completely, but rather, deciding how and when to engage. For example, you might opt to only discuss light topics during family gatherings or suggest taking breaks if conversations become heated. Understanding that you have the right to avoid these energy-draining situations can significantly lessen your feelings of anxiety.

Addressing Work Issues

Work-related pressures can often be a source of anxiety for many people. For example, suppose you have a job that comes with a lot of expectations from your employer or even from yourself. When the pressure to perform is high, it can sometimes feel overwhelming.

It is important to recognize these feelings and find ways to manage them effectively. Here are some suggestions to consider:

- **Break down work tasks into smaller manageable tasks.** If you have a large project that's due in a week, you can start by outlining all the components that need to be completed and creating a list of these smaller tasks so that you can focus on one thing at a time. This method not only helps in reducing anxiety but also provides a clear path forward.

- **Set work priorities.** When faced with many tasks, it can be helpful to identify which ones require immediate attention and which can wait. For example, if you have a deadline for a report in two days, that task should take precedence over other less urgent tasks such as responding to emails. By focusing on what is most important first, you can alleviate some of the pressure on your shoulders.

- **Address time management issues.** Try to allocate specific time slots for each task, which can help you stay organized and focused. For instance, if you decide to spend two hours on research, set a timer. This creates a sense of urgency that can enhance productivity. If distractions arise, such as phone notifications or social media, try to minimize these by using apps that block distracting websites during your designated work time. Learning to manage your time effectively is key to reducing anxiety and meeting work expectations.

- **Invest in self-care.** Engaging in regular physical activity can significantly impact your overall well-being. For example, you might consider taking short breaks to go for a walk. Just stepping outside and breathing in fresh air can help clear your mind and provide a moment of relief. When you return to work, you will feel refreshed and ready to get back to your tasks. Furthermore, establishing a routine that includes regular meals, sufficient sleep, and relaxation time is essential. The aim is to be consistent with healthy habits rather than overcommitting to habits that you cannot sustain in the long term. Thus, think of small but impactful ways of enhancing your physical and mental health every day.

- **Seek ongoing support to manage stress.** Talking to colleagues, friends, or family can provide emotional relief and practical solutions. For example, if you feel stuck on a project, discussing it with a trusted coworker might offer new perspectives and ideas. Sometimes, just sharing feelings of anxiety can lighten the load. It's worth noting that many workplaces offer resources such as counseling services or workshops on stress management. Taking advantage of these options can empower you to handle work pressures more effectively.

Guilt: Handling Feelings of Unmet Expectations

From a young age, you may have found yourself in positions that required you to take on a lot of responsibility. This may have created a sense of guilt when you think you haven't met the expectations placed upon you.

Society adds another layer to this issue. Women in general are often expected to uphold certain standards. We often hear phrases like "a nurturing mother" or "a supportive partner." These ideals pressure you to be kind, selfless, and giving. You may do your best to embody these traits but fail to achieve them sometimes, which is normal. When this happens, though, guilt can seep into your life.

The cycle of these feelings can feel never-ending. When there are so many demands, failing to meet just one can feel like a disaster. Imagine a scenario where there is an important deadline at work, coinciding with a family event that you are supposed to attend. Having to choose one over the other can lead to guilt regardless of the choice you end up making. If you choose work, you might feel bad about not being with your family. If you choose family, you may worry about your job. This constant juggling act can create a heavy burden of guilt that feels impossible to escape.

In the journey to handle these feelings, it's important to identify ways to let go of guilt. Below are some strategies you can practice whenever you are caught between choosing yourself and meeting family obligations.

Recognize Your Limits

Recognizing that everyone has limits is crucial. You need to understand that you cannot always be available for everyone while simultaneously focusing on your personal development. Setting boundaries is not just a nice concept; it is a necessary action for your mental well-being. For instance, whenever you feel overwhelmed by family duties assigned to you, communicate your need for help or let go of specific responsibilities temporarily. Remind yourself that it's okay to ask for assistance from family members or delegate tasks. This sharing of responsibilities can lighten the emotional load and create a more equal distribution of duties within your family.

Practice Self-Compassion

It's essential for you to be kind to yourself in times when you feel overstretched. Treat yourself the same way you would treat a dear friend. Instead of finding fault in your thoughts and feelings, take a moment to reflect on the stress you may be under. You could also take time each week to acknowledge positive contributions you are making in various relationships and areas of your life such as your work, health, and goals. Write down the achievements or activities that made you feel proud or competent so that you have a tangible reminder of what you have done well.

Set Realistic Goals

Setting achievable goals, rather than trying to be perfect in all areas, can help you manage your expectations. You can choose to focus on specific achievements that align with your personal values and measure success on your terms instead of someone else's standards. For instance, if you value solitude but also want to spend time with your family during the week or month, schedule quality time without overexerting yourself. Or, if you value financial stability but also want to support your family financially, decide how much money you can contribute to your family's needs without compromising your own financial needs.

Furthermore, understanding that guilt often stems from a place of care encourages eldest daughters to see things from a different perspective. When you feel guilty about not fulfilling a role, reframe this feeling as an opportunity for self-growth to change the narrative. It might be helpful to view such moments as lessons rather than failures. This shift in mentality can open the door to healthier coping strategies.

Therefore, approaching feelings of guilt is not just about eliminating them but about understanding their sources and finding friendly ways to cope. Finding a support group or trusted friends who share similar experiences can also provide a sense of relief. Sharing personal stories can highlight common challenges and bring about a sense of community. It normalizes feelings of guilt and makes it easier to manage them.

Ultimately, guilt is a common emotion for many eldest daughters, and understanding its origins is the first step toward managing it. Exploring methods to reduce guilt through realistic expectations, self-compassion, and a supportive community can lead to a more fulfilling experience.

Ultimately, balancing responsibilities with personal needs is key. It is important to acknowledge that everyone's path is different and that it's okay to strive for balance in life.

Shame: Exploring Deep-Rooted Emotional Responses

Shame is an intense feeling that many eldest daughters encounter as they grow up. It can be a silent force that affects their lives in various ways. This emotion often relates to feelings of unworthiness, which might arise due to external judgments or expectations from family and society. For instance, you might feel overwhelmed by the need to live up to the high standards set by your parents. This pressure could lead you to believe that anything less than perfection is unacceptable. Over time, these feelings can create a persistent sense of shame that impacts your confidence and self-image.

Shame is different from guilt, even though people often confuse the two. Guilt usually arises from a specific action that someone regrets. For example, if you forget to call your mother on your birthday, you might feel guilty for not being there. In this case, guilt encourages you to make amends. You might apologize and make plans to celebrate your mother's birthday at a later date.

As you can see, there are some positive benefits for feeling guilty. This emotion can sometimes foster positive change or repair broken relationships, serving as a reminder that our actions matter and can motivate us to do better next time.

On the other hand, shame takes a broader approach. It is not tied to a particular action, but instead relates to how a person perceives themselves as a whole. When you feel shame, you think that you are flawed or defective. For example, you might internalize your family's high expectations and develop the belief that you are not enough, no matter how hard you try to gain skills and improve your life. This feeling can lead you to withdraw from social interactions or avoid situations where you feel judged. Thus, shame does more harm than good. In many cases, shame makes people feel as if they must hide parts of themselves to be accepted.

Moreover, shame can diminish your ability to empathize with others. When you are focused so intently on your perceived flaws, it becomes challenging to connect with or understand what others are going through. For example, grappling with shame could make it difficult for you to support a friend in distress because you are preoccupied with your own feelings of inadequacy. This lack of connection can create a barrier in friendships and lead to feelings of loneliness. For this reason, it is essential to recognize how shame affects your relationships and to find ways to counteract its influence.

Neither guilt nor shame is healthy when felt over long periods. While both emotions can be a natural part of being human, dwelling on them can lead to mental health challenges. Acknowledging when shame arises can be the first step toward dealing with it effectively.

Several strategies can help individuals cope with shame, and building self-compassion is one of the most effective methods to do so. Self-compassion, as described above, involves treating yourself with kindness and understanding, especially during difficult times. Rather than criticizing yourself for not meeting expectations, it encourages you to recognize your humanity.

Openly discuss your feelings with trusted friends, family members, or even professionals who can provide relief. Sharing experiences and thoughts with others can help diminish the power of shame over you. It reminds you that you are not alone in your feelings and that others may have similar experiences. This realization can create connections that replace feelings of isolation with support and understanding.

It may be beneficial to challenge negative thoughts that arise from shame. When feelings of inadequacy take over, asking yourself if those thoughts are based on facts can be helpful. It's also essential to distinguish between facts and the stories you tell yourself. For instance, you may feel like a failure in your caregiving duties, but examining your achievements and personal growth can provide a more balanced view. This step can help counteract the harsh narrative that shame promotes.

Spotting Burnout Before It's Too Late

Burnout is a pressing issue that many eldest daughters face. We can define burnout as the state of physical, mental, and emotional exhaustion that occurs after a prolonged period of chronic stress.

Identifying when you are experiencing burnout involves understanding its manifestations. Physical symptoms such as chronic fatigue, headaches, and gastrointestinal issues are common indicators. Emotional signs include feelings of overwhelming stress, irritability, and a pervasive sense of helplessness (WebMD Editorial Contributor, 2024). You might also have trouble concentrating, a lack of motivation, or a sense of entrapment in your roles.

Once you have identified these signs, it's important to act immediately to avoid further decline into severe burnout. Note that some signs may be subtle and seem like "normal" stress symptoms. This is why it's vital to pay attention to how your body and mind respond to daily pressures. What may appear like temporary stress could be signs of a more significant problem. For instance, you might brush off persistent fatigue as simply being "tired," but it's essential to recognize when this tiredness becomes debilitating and impacts your daily functioning.

Strategies for recovery from burnout encompass various approaches centered on self-care. Incorporate breaks and personal check-ins into your daily schedule. Stepping away from sources of stress periodically to focus on your well-being can prevent the escalation of burnout. Regularly ask yourself questions like, "How am I doing emotionally?" and "How am I doing physically?" so you can stay connected with your needs and take timely action to address them.

Recovering from burnout requires intentional efforts to recalibrate your life and establish routines that promote well-being. Your personal health shouldn't be sacrificed for the sake of your responsibilities. Striking a balance is essential for long-term sustainability and avoiding future burnout episodes. Remember to communicate openly with your support system about your struggles and needs in order to alleviate the burden of carrying your responsibilities alone.

Professional Stress Management Options

Professional help can be extraordinarily beneficial for those struggling with persistent anxiety, guilt, shame, and burnout. This type of support comes in many forms and is available for anyone who struggles to resolve emotional issues on their own.

Psychotherapy

Talking to a licensed therapist or counselor can provide you with a deeper understanding of your experiences and equip you with coping strategies tailored to your specific needs. On a practical level, therapy can help you reframe negative thought patterns, set realistic expectations for yourself, and develop healthier ways of relating to your family.

Cognitive Behavioral Therapy

Cognitive behavioral therapy (CBT) focuses on changing unhelpful thinking and behavior patterns. Through CBT, you can learn to challenge unrealistic expectations and adopt a more balanced perspective. This can be particularly useful if you have internalized the belief that you must always be perfect and responsible for everyone else's happiness.

Schema Therapy

Schema therapy is a type of talk therapy that addresses long-standing cognitive and behavioral patterns by uncovering the cause behind them. It goes beyond changing your thoughts, as is the case with CBT, but in this case, by actually uprooting the schema or "mental model" that has led to that thinking. Moreover, schema therapy can help you cultivate self-compassion and recognize your worth beyond your family roles.

Learning to Say "Yes" (to Yourself)

As the eldest daughter, you're probably used to saying "yes" to everyone else. "Yes" to helping with the younger siblings, "yes" to taking on extra responsibilities, and "yes" to being the family's go-to problem solver. But how often do you say "yes" to yourself?

It's easy to get caught up in the whirlwind of obligations, but it's essential to remember that your needs, dreams, and well-being are just as important as those of the people you care for. In this section, we'll explore the art of unapologetically saying "yes" to yourself with a touch of humor and a whole lot of empowerment.

Saying "Yes" to "Me Time"

Picture this: You've just finished organizing yet another family event, and everyone's happy—but you're drained. Instead of diving into the next task, imagine saying, "Yes, I deserve a break." Grab that book, take a long bath, or binge-watch your favorite series guilt-free. The world won't collapse if you take a little time for yourself. In fact, you might find that when you return, you're more refreshed, recharged, and ready to tackle whatever comes next.

Affirming Statement: *My family may need me, but I need myself more.*

Saying "Yes" to Your Dreams

Remember that passion project or dream career you've always put on the back burner? It's time to bring it to the front. Whether it's writing a novel, starting a small business, or traveling solo, give yourself permission to say "yes" to whatever lights you up. Your dreams are just as important as everyone else's, and pursuing them isn't selfish—rather, it's necessary for your fulfillment and happiness.

Affirming Statement: *I have helped everyone else reach their goals; now it's my turn.*

Saying "Yes" to Limits

Setting limits can feel like a foreign concept, especially when you're used to being everything to everyone. But saying "yes" to limits means giving yourself the space to breathe and the freedom to focus on what truly matters to you. Whether it's declining a request that's too much or carving out time in your schedule for personal projects, embracing limits is a powerful way to protect your energy and prioritize your well-being.

Affirming Statement: *It's okay for me to say "no" to others so I can say "yes" to myself.*

Saying "Yes" to Fun

When was the last time you did something just for fun? As the eldest daughter, you've mastered the art of responsibility—but don't forget to embrace your playful side. Whether it's dancing like no one's watching, indulging in a spontaneous adventure, or laughing until your sides hurt, saying "yes" to fun is saying "yes" to living a balanced, joyful life. After all, you deserve to experience happiness in its purest form.

Affirming Statement: *Life isn't just about responsibilities; it's about joy, too.*

Saying "Yes" to Self-Compassion

Perfection is overrated, and mistakes are part of the journey. Instead of being your harshest critic, try being your biggest supporter. When things don't go as planned, say "yes" to self-compassion. Remind yourself that you're doing the best you can, and that's more than enough. Embracing your humanity, flaws and all, is a beautiful way to show yourself the love and understanding you so freely give to others.

Affirming Statement: *I'm allowed to be kind to myself, even when I stumble.*

By saying "yes" to these aspects of your life, you're not only nurturing your own happiness but also setting a powerful example for others. It's a reminder that you deserve to be at the top of your own priority list, and that's something worth celebrating.

Concluding Thoughts

In this chapter, we explored how anxiety, burnout, guilt, and shame can impact eldest daughters. These emotions often stem from high expectations and responsibilities within the family.

Embracing the strategies offered in this chapter promotes emotional resilience and leads to a more balanced, fulfilling life. Furthermore, understanding that healing is a gradual process allows for greater patience and perseverance along the way.

The next chapter focuses on the power of creativity and personal exploration as tools to help eldest daughters break free from the restrictive roles often imposed on them. It encourages embracing spontaneity, rediscovering passions, and building a more playful, authentic life.

"When one door of happiness closes, another opens; but often we look so long at the closed door that we do not see the one which has been opened for us."

Helen Keller

Chapter 7
Breaking the Cycle of Self-Neglect

Rewrite Your Life Narrative

Breaking the cycle of restrictive roles involves embracing creativity and personal exploration, proactively stepping away from the expectations that have long since defined your life, and rediscovering the passions and spontaneity that bring you authentic joy. This chapter looks into the journey of reigniting your playful spirit and creating a lifestyle where responsibilities do not overshadow your individuality.

Rewriting your life narrative is a powerful first step toward empowering yourself. Consider how you communicate your stories to others. The way we articulate our experiences can highlight our growth or keep us stuck in a victim mentality.

Audibly telling your story to a friend or writing it down can also assist in understanding it better. Each retelling allows you to emphasize parts of the narrative that reflect strength and resilience. Instead of saying, "I lost my job," you could say, "I learned valuable lessons from the experience of losing my job, which helped me to understand what I truly want in my career." This subtle shift in language can significantly impact your sense of self and the way others perceive your journey.

Ultimately, your stories about being an eldest daughter should reflect your true self and the humanity of your experiences. Reclaiming agency over your identity means taking back the power from expectations and narratives that do not serve you.

Begin today by identifying one aspect of your life that feels particularly restrictive. Ask yourself why it feels that way and how you might view it differently. Maybe you feel pressured to pursue a particular career path because of family expectations. Challenge this notion by researching other career options or pursuing interests that truly excite you, even if they differ from traditional expectations. Engaging in this deeper exploration allows you to face those external pressures and consider how to honor your true self in the process.

Embarking on this journey to rewrite your life narrative requires more than just changing your perspective; it requires crafting a life that feels meaningful to you. The path ahead is about rediscovery and embracing what makes your life unique—a narrative that shines a light on your individuality while breaking free from the constraints of roles that have held you back for too long.

Techniques for Reshaping Personal Stories

Rewriting personal narratives can be a powerful way to reflect on your life's experiences and communicate them more effectively. This process involves various techniques that can help you clarify your thoughts and feelings while putting a positive twist on your stories.

Examples of the techniques you can use include

- **Journaling:** This allows you to take a step back, analyze your experiences, and assign new meanings to them. For example, instead of viewing a challenging period solely as a time of hardship, it can be reinterpreted as a phase of significant personal growth. Yes, it may have been a painful period in your life, but the value is that it revealed hidden strengths and qualities about you that you wouldn't have discovered otherwise. Journaling transforms raw emotions into structured thoughts, providing more clarity and alternative perspectives about your life circumstances, which can allow you to feel a sense of control over your story.

- **Narrative therapy:** This form of therapy encourages you to detach from your problems by externalizing them. Developed by therapists Michael White and David Epston, this technique helps separate the person from their issues, making it easier to address challenges without feeling personally diminished by them (Clarke, 2023). For instance, whenever you feel overwhelmed by family obligations, you can learn to see these pressures as external factors that you can choose to subscribe to or unsubscribe to, rather than intrinsic flaws. This detachment empowers you to challenge these dynamics more effectively.

- **Deconstruction therapy:** Therapists also employ deconstruction, where stories are broken down into smaller, manageable parts. This approach helps you gain a clearer understanding of your narratives without feeling lost in overarching negative themes. Deconstructing a story can reveal underlying patterns and pinpoint specific events that had significant impacts, allowing for targeted reframing and healing.

- **Imagining alternative outcomes:** Think about the many ways in which the inconveniences of your life could be reimagined to emphasize positive and empowering possibilities. For example, when you say no to funding an unexpected family financial emergency, imagine the positive ways in which the situation might unfold. Perhaps your parents and siblings may combine resources and pay the expense, or maybe a surprise donation or financial gift is given to a family member that helps to fund the expense. The act of envisioning different futures builds resilience and shifts your focus from what could go wrong to what could go right, thereby cultivating hope and motivation.

Learn to Articulate Your Stories

When you learn to express your narratives clearly and confidently, you regain control over how others perceive them. Sharing your personal stories can be done through writing, speaking, or even creative outlets like art and music. These means of expression can not only validate your experiences but also encourage self-compassion and greater empathy and understanding from others.

You may hold the story that your childhood was consumed by caretaking duties. By sharing your story, you can highlight the sacrifices you made, and the skills developed through the role you played within your family. This articulation not only helps you process your feelings but also educates others about the unique challenges faced by eldest daughters. As you courageously communicate your journey, you will transform from a passive participant in your life to an active narrator with a voice that commands respect and recognition.

Frame Your Experiences Positively

Positive framing of experiences is a powerful tool for empowerment. Rather than dwelling on the limitations imposed by your family roles, you can focus on the strengths and growth that emerged from your responsibilities. This isn't meant to downplay the silent struggles you have been through but instead serves as a way for you to reconcile your past with your present and move forward.

For instance, managing household tasks from a young age may have brought several disadvantages like maturing too soon or missing out on innocent childhood experiences. However, on the other hand, this same experience might have taught you exceptional organizational skills and resilience. Recognizing these positives allows for a more balanced perspective that celebrates strengths rather than focusing solely on burdens.

Tim Wilson's research on "story editing" and "story prompting" techniques illustrates the benefit of positive reframing (Rutledge, 2016). By identifying and altering harmful narratives, you can shift your mindset from one of defeat to one of empowerment. This mental shift is essential for long-term well-being and personal growth. For instance, if you previously saw yourself as merely dutiful, you may begin to view yourself as a warm and loving person to be around, thereby breaking free from the restrictive, one-dimensional perspective of yourself.

Shift Your Language From Obligation to Empowerment

The language you use shapes your perceptions and interactions. By shifting from a language of obligation to one of empowerment, you can significantly alter your experience of your roles. Instead of saying, "I have to take care of my siblings," you can reframe it as "I choose to support my family because it aligns with my values." This subtle change empowers you to perceive your actions as choices rather than imposed duties, creating a sense of autonomy and satisfaction.

Language plays a critical role in your daily affirmations and self-talk as well. Phrases like "I am trapped in this role" can be transformed into "I have the strength and resourcefulness to navigate my responsibilities." This shift not only enhances self-perception but also influences how you interact with others. It can also promote more assertive and confident communication.

Incorporating positive language into your everyday life requires practice and mindfulness. A great place to start is by identifying phrases that feel disempowering and consciously replacing them with empowering alternatives. Over time, this practice becomes second nature, leading to a more optimistic and proactive outlook.

Embrace Playfulness and Rediscovering Your Joy

Reconnecting with one's playful, creative side can be a transformative experience for eldest daughters, who often bear the weight of family expectations and responsibilities. Embracing spontaneity and joy is essential in breaking free from restrictive roles and cultivating a more balanced, joyful existence.

Integrating playfulness into your daily life can have profound effects on both your mental and physical well-being. Play isn't just for children—adults can also benefit significantly from engaging in playful activities. According to research, adult play boosts creativity, sharpens humor, and helps cope better with stress (Des Marais, 2022). Imagine taking an impromptu dance break in your living room or playing a lighthearted game of tag with friends. These moments of play can alleviate stress, promote relaxation, and improve overall life satisfaction.

Play introduces a state of mind where you are fully absorbed in an enjoyable activity, losing track of time and setting aside your worries. This mental shift can create a sense of balance, making it easier to handle daily stresses and responsibilities. Think about how children prioritize play, devoting time each day to activities that bring them joy. As adults, we should strive to adopt this mindset, integrating playful moments into our routines as acts of self-care.

Creative Outlets

Engaging in creative pursuits like art, music, or dance allows for self-expression and enjoyment without the need for perfection. Many eldest daughters feel pressured to excel in every area of their lives, leaving little room for pursuits that do not have tangible outcomes. However, pursuing creative outlets can be incredibly liberating. For instance, painting a simple landscape or learning to play an instrument provides a space to explore new interests and express emotions freely.

Encouraging hobbies without the pressure to achieve excellence is vital. Consider joining a local art class or taking up knitting. The aim isn't to create a masterpiece but to enjoy the process and find solace in the act of creation. When you engage in artistic endeavors, the focus shifts from performance to expression, helping you reconnect with your authentic self.

Spontaneous Adventures

Saying "yes" to unexpected opportunities can help you break out of routine and rediscover your sense of wonder. It is common for life to become a series of planned and predictable events, leaving little room for spontaneity. Yet, some of the most enriching experiences come from unplanned adventures.

Whether it's honoring an unexpected invitation to a camping trip or visiting a nearby city you've never explored, stepping out of your comfort zone and doing something different can lead to unforgettable memories and a renewed appreciation for life's unpredictability. These spontaneous adventures inject excitement into your everyday life, encouraging a break from monotony and rigidity. With that said, you don't need to wait for an invitation to give yourself permission to be spontaneous. Plan an outing at least once a month that deviates from your normal routine and lets you meet new people or try new experiences.

Pursuing Activities Without Perfection

It's essential to emphasize again that enjoyment and expression do not require mastery or success. As we have discussed in earlier chapters, the pursuit of perfection can be overwhelming. However, embracing activities simply for the joy they bring can be a refreshing change. Try gardening without worrying about growing the perfect plants or baking without aiming for flawless results. Engage in hobbies where the journey is more important than the destination and remind yourself that it's okay to be imperfect. What matters most is enjoying yourself and exploring new facets of your personality.

Cultivating Curiosity and Expanding Horizons

Curiosity is a powerful force that can drive personal growth and open up new vistas in life. Eldest daughters, often bound by expectations and roles within the family, can benefit immensely from cultivating curiosity and exploring new interests and perspectives. This journey begins with lifelong learning—a commitment to continuously absorb knowledge through various channels such as reading, taking classes, or traveling.

Embracing Lifelong Learning

Lifelong learning encourages you to step beyond your familiar world and engage with new ideas, ultimately broadening your horizons and challenging existing beliefs. Take, for instance, the simple act of reading a book by an author from a different culture. The narratives, traditions, and philosophies you encounter can challenge your preconceptions and expand your worldview. Classes and educational programs, whether online or in-person, offer structured learning experiences that not only impart knowledge but also encourage critical thinking. Traveling, perhaps more than any other activity, can significantly alter one's perspective by showing firsthand how diverse and multifaceted human life can be.

Lifelong learning involves acquiring, applying, and reflecting on knowledge. Every new piece of information should be examined in the context of your existing beliefs and experiences. Reflecting on and discussing what you've learned with others can deepen your understanding and make the knowledge more relevant to your life.

Being Curious About New Perspectives

Exploring new perspectives is another crucial aspect of breaking the cycle of restrictive roles. Engaging with diverse ideas and cultures about eldest daughters, or family dynamics in general, can be incredibly enriching. This might mean participating in cultural events, attending lectures on unfamiliar subjects, or simply having conversations with people who have different backgrounds and viewpoints than you do.

Stepping outside your comfort zone is key here. When you engage with differing perspectives, you are less likely to conform to traditional roles because you realize that there are numerous ways to live and think. This can reduce the pressure to meet specific expectations and allow you to carve out a more authentic path for yourself.

For example, consider joining a discussion group that focuses on contemporary social issues affecting women or families. By hearing varied opinions and engaging in debates, you not only broaden your understanding of these issues but also learn to appreciate the diversity of thought. This practice can help in reducing the internalized pressure to conform to any particular norm, which expands your view of life.

Embracing a Beginner's Mindset

Adopting a beginner's mindset is equally important. This involves embracing the idea that it's perfectly okay to be a novice at something new. Often, eldest daughters feel the weight of responsibility and expertise, believing that they must excel in everything they undertake. However, allowing yourself to be a beginner opens up avenues for growth without the burden of expertise or responsibility.

Be willing to make mistakes and learn from every setback. This approach not only enriches your life with new skills and experiences but also alleviates the stress of constant perfection. In a family setting, this beginner's mindset can translate into being more open to learning from younger siblings or even children. It can create a more balanced dynamic where the exchange of knowledge and experiences flows both ways, making family relationships richer and more equitable.

Questioning Your Beliefs

Challenging existing beliefs is essential for developing more personalized viewpoints. Many eldest daughters grow up adhering to inherited norms and values without questioning their relevance or validity. Encouraging self-inquiry and critical thinking can liberate you from these constraints and allow you to form beliefs that truly resonate with your individual identity.

Questioning inherited beliefs doesn't mean rejecting them outright. Rather, it's about examining why you hold certain views and determining if they align with your authentic self. For instance, if you were raised to prioritize duty and responsibility above all else, you might begin to question this belief at this juncture in your life and explore the value of self-care and personal fulfillment. This process can lead to a more balanced and holistic approach to life where you honor your commitments while also nurturing your own well-being.

Engaging in discussions with friends, mentors, or counselors can be immensely helpful in this regard. They can provide different perspectives and challenge you to think more deeply about your beliefs. Reflective journaling is another effective tool for examining and reshaping your viewpoints.

Celebrating Individuality and Honoring Your True Self

Embracing your unique qualities and quirks as an eldest daughter begins with recognizing that what sets you apart is not a hindrance but a gift. Often, eldest daughters face the pressure of conforming to expectations set by family, society, or even self-imposed standards. However, stepping into your uniqueness can be immensely liberating.

Embracing Uniqueness

Celebrating what makes you different starts by shifting your perspective from seeking validation through conformity to finding strength in individuality. It's common for eldest daughters to feel the need to fulfill roles assigned to them—whether it may be caretaker, overachiever, or peacemaker. These roles often overshadow personal aspirations and authenticity. However, when you start to see your unique traits as strengths rather than oddities, you free yourself from those restricting labels.

See yourself as a mosaic made up of various experiences, talents, and quirks. Each piece contributes to the whole picture that is uniquely you. Embrace the parts of you that stand out, whether it's your sense of humor, your distinctive fashion sense, or an unusual hobby. These differences add color to your life and narrative.

Consider writing down aspects of your personality that you've been told are "different" or "odd." Reflect on how they contribute positively to your life and relationships. This exercise helps in reframing your mindset to appreciate, rather than suppress, these traits.

Personal Rituals

Creating and honoring personal rituals can serve as powerful affirmations of your identity. Personal rituals are small, daily practices that resonate deeply with who you are and what you value. They act as anchors, helping to reinforce a strong sense of self, especially when external demands become overwhelming.

Begin by identifying activities that bring you joy or peace. Whether it's a morning run, a moment of meditation, or journaling before bed, these rituals should reflect your tastes and preferences. Consistency in these practices nurtures your soul and keeps you grounded in your authenticity. If you love nature, consider making a ritual out of a weekly hike or gardening session. If music moves you, perhaps setting aside time to play an instrument or listen to a favorite album can serve as a personal sanctuary. The key is to make these rituals nonnegotiable parts of your routine, thus continuously acknowledging and reaffirming your individuality.

Honoring Your Journey

Every milestone, no matter how small, is worth celebrating. Eldest daughters often bear the weight of high expectations, leading them to overlook their own achievements in favor of striving for the next goal. Honoring your journey involves recognizing both big accomplishments and small victories, understanding that each step forward is a testament to your growth and resilience.

Create a habit of acknowledging your progress. Keep a journal where you note down your achievements, however minor they may seem. Did you manage to assert yourself in a difficult conversation? Write it down. Did you complete a project at work? Celebrate that! This practice not only builds a positive record of your efforts but also serves as a reminder of your capabilities during challenging times.

Visual reminders can also be helpful. Set up a dedicated space in your home where you display mementos of your achievements. This could include awards, photos, or even simple notes to yourself. Each item acts as a tangible recognition of your journey, reminding you of the distance you've covered and the strength you've shown.

Building Confidence

Confidence isn't about being flawless; it's about embracing your strengths and showing up as your authentic self despite imperfections. To build confidence, focus on practices that highlight your personal strengths and reinforce your self-worth. Recognize that your abilities, character, and values are unique contributions only you can offer.

Start by listing your strengths. Are you a natural leader? Do you have a knack for problem-solving? Are you empathetic and supportive? Writing these down reinforces a positive self-image and provides a reference point whenever self-doubt creeps in. Next, engage in activities that leverage these strengths. If you excel in organizing events, volunteer to plan a community gathering or a family celebration. If you're good at writing, start a blog or contribute articles that reflect your passions and insights. These actions not only bolster your confidence but also create opportunities for others to recognize and appreciate your talents.

Surround yourself with a supportive community. Seek out friends, mentors, or groups that celebrate and encourage your authentic self. Positive reinforcement from others can significantly boost your confidence and help you stay committed to your path of self-acceptance. Lastly, understand that setbacks and mistakes are part of the journey, not a reflection of your worth.

The Eldest Daughter's Playlist

Sometimes, you need a soundtrack that reflects the unique journey you're on—one that empowers, uplifts, and even brings a smile to your face. Enter *The Eldest Daughter's Playlist*, a collection of songs that perfectly captures the spirit of eldest daughters everywhere. These tracks are more than just music; they're anthems that resonate deeply with the experiences of balancing expectations, embracing self-compassion, and finding the courage to be yourself.

"Woman" by Doja Cat

This track is a celebration of the multifaceted nature of womanhood. Eldest daughters often find themselves juggling various roles—caregiver, leader, mediator—much like the song's portrayal of women as powerful and capable in every aspect of life. The upbeat, confident vibe of "Woman" encourages eldest daughters to embrace their strength and resilience, reminding them of their ability to handle whatever comes their way.

"Break My Soul" by Beyoncé

This song is an anthem of liberation and empowerment, encouraging listeners to break free from the pressures and expectations that weigh them down. For eldest daughters, who often feel the burden of responsibility and obligation, "Break My Soul" is a powerful reminder that it's okay to prioritize their own well-being and seek freedom from societal and familial demands. The message of resilience and self-empowerment resonates deeply with those looking to reclaim their lives and identities.

"Good as Hell" by Lizzo

Lizzo's "Good as Hell" is all about self-love and confidence—two things that eldest daughters might struggle to maintain when they're constantly focused on taking care of others. This upbeat anthem encourages them to put themselves first and recognize their own value, offering a much-needed boost of positivity and self-affirmation. The song's infectious energy makes it the perfect pick-me-up for those moments when eldest daughters need to remind themselves that they're doing an amazing job.

"Sorry Not Sorry" by Demi Lovato

This track is all about unapologetically standing up for yourself and not being sorry for prioritizing your own needs and happiness. Eldest daughters, who might feel guilty for putting themselves first, will find empowerment in this song's bold message. It's a declaration of self-confidence and a reminder that it's okay to be proud of who you are and what you've accomplished.

"Shake It Off" by Taylor Swift

"Shake It Off" is a fun, upbeat song that encourages listeners to let go of negativity and embrace their true selves. For eldest daughters, who might face criticism or feel weighed down by expectations, it is a perfect reminder to release stress and not let others' opinions get in the way of their happiness. The song's carefree energy serves as a perfect antidote to the pressures eldest daughters often face.

Each of these songs is a celebration of the strength, courage, and unique journey of eldest daughters. They serve as both a soundtrack and a source of inspiration, offering motivation to embrace who you are and live your life with a sense of joy and empowerment. So turn up the volume, let these anthems fill your space, and remember: You're not just the eldest daughter; you're the author of your own story.

Concluding Thoughts

This chapter revealed the value of creativity and personal exploration in helping eldest daughters break free from restrictive roles. By embracing spontaneity and integrating playfulness into daily life, eldest daughters can cultivate a more balanced and joyful existence. Techniques such as journaling, narrative therapy, and positive reframing are effective strategies for reshaping personal stories and building a more empowering mindset.

The next chapter aims to share anecdotes and case studies of experiences and insights from eldest daughters, highlighting diverse backgrounds, challenges faced, lessons learned, and unique insights that reveal common themes and differences among their journeys.

> *"We need to accept that we won't always make the right decisions, that we'll screw up royally sometimes. Understanding that failure is not the opposite of success, it's part of success."*
>
> Arianna Huffington

Chapter 8
Uplifting Stories From Eldest Daughters

How Our Diverse Backgrounds Shape Our Childhoods

Sharing the experiences of eldest daughters from various backgrounds uncovers the intricate layers of their roles and responsibilities. These stories, drawn from diverse cultural, socioeconomic, and educational contexts, paint a vivid picture of what it means to navigate family dynamics as the firstborn daughter. Each narrative highlights unique challenges and poignant moments, offering glimpses into how these women manage expectations while striving for personal fulfillment.

In sharing the experiences of eldest daughters from diverse cultural and socioeconomic backgrounds, we unearth a vast array of stories that depict the multifaceted nature of their roles. These narratives not only highlight the unique challenges faced by eldest daughters but also offer an in-depth understanding of how varied influences shape their lives.

Navigating Different Cultural Norms and Expectations

Eldest daughters often navigate expectations and pressures that are deeply rooted in their cultural backgrounds. However, not all families subscribe to traditional values, meaning that not all eldest daughters will grow up being exposed to some of these pressures. Here are stories that illustrate how cultural norms and variations can influence family dynamics and the expectations placed on the eldest daughters.

Sara's Journey Through Tradition and Responsibility

Sara, an eldest daughter in a South Asian family, grew up with the weight of her cultural heritage resting firmly on her shoulders. In her family, traditional values were paramount, and as the eldest daughter, Sara was expected to embody these traditions fully.

From a young age, she was tasked with caring for her younger siblings, managing household chores, and even taking on the emotional labor of keeping the family together. In her culture, these responsibilities were seen as essential training for her future roles as a wife and mother. Sara often found herself sacrificing her own interests and ambitions to fulfill these duties, while her younger brothers were encouraged to focus on their studies and interests.

As she grew older, Sara began to feel the tension between her cultural responsibilities and her personal dreams. While she loved her family deeply, she also yearned for more freedom to explore her own passions. Navigating this complex terrain required Sara to find a delicate balance between honoring her cultural heritage and asserting her right to pursue her own life goals. Her journey highlights the profound impact that traditional cultural expectations can have on the roles and identities of eldest daughters.

Rina's Experience with Egalitarian Values

Rina grew up in a Scandinavian country known for its strong emphasis on gender equality. As the eldest daughter, she was aware of her role within the family, but the expectations placed upon her were markedly different from those of Sara. In Rina's culture, the division of labor was more balanced, with all siblings, regardless of gender, sharing household responsibilities equally.

Rina's parents encouraged her to pursue her own interests and passions, just as they did with her brothers. There was no assumption that she, as the eldest daughter, should take on more caregiving duties or sacrifice her ambitions for the sake of her family. Instead, Rina was free to focus on her studies, engage in extracurricular activities, and plan for her future. This egalitarian approach allowed her to develop a strong sense of independence and self-confidence.

Rina's experience illustrates how cultural beliefs about equality can significantly influence the roles and opportunities available to eldest daughters, granting them greater freedom to define their own paths.

Mei's Bridge Between Tradition and Modernity

Mei's story is one of cultural transition and adaptation. Born in rural China, Mei was raised with traditional values that emphasized academic achievement and strict gender roles. As the eldest daughter, she was expected to excel in school while also helping with household chores and caring for her younger siblings. Her parents, like many in their community, believed that these responsibilities would prepare Mei for a successful future, both academically and domestically.

However, when Mei's family emigrated to Canada, the cultural landscape around them began to change. Living in an urban, multicultural environment exposed Mei's parents to different perspectives on gender roles and parenting. Over time, they began to adopt more westernized views, encouraging Mei to embrace independence and self-expression. This shift in parental attitudes allowed Mei to explore interests beyond academics and caregiving such as art and sports, which she had previously set aside.

Mei's experience reflects the complex dynamics that arise when traditional cultural expectations intersect with modern, globalized values. As the eldest daughter, she found herself at the crossroads of these two worlds, learning to navigate the expectations of her heritage while also embracing the opportunities offered by her new environment. Mei's story highlights the adaptability and resilience required of eldest daughters, who must often bridge the gap between tradition and modernity within their families.

The Haves and the Have-Nots: How Socioeconomic Factors Influence Eldest Daughter Experiences

The economic status of a family greatly influences the responsibilities and opportunities afforded to eldest daughters. In low-income households, eldest daughters might bear greater burdens than their counterparts from wealthier families. These contrasting realities underscore how economic status shapes the experiences of eldest daughters, influencing not only their immediate roles within the family but also their long-term opportunities and life trajectories. Here are a few stories that illustrate the difference that socioeconomic factors can make in shaping eldest daughters' realities and opportunities.

Maria's Journey in Brazil

Maria grew up in a small town in Brazil, where her family struggled to make ends meet. As the eldest daughter in a low-income household, Maria's role was defined not just by her birth order but by the economic realities her family faced. Her parents worked long hours at low-paying jobs, barely earning enough to cover basic necessities. By the time Maria was 14, it became clear that her family needed her to contribute financially.

Maria had always excelled in school, but the dream of continuing her education was overshadowed by the immediate needs of her family. She made the difficult decision to drop out of school and take on multiple jobs—cleaning houses in the mornings, working at a local market in the afternoons, and caring for her younger siblings in the evenings. Her days were long and exhausting, but she took pride in knowing that her efforts helped keep her family afloat.

However, the weight of her responsibilities was heavy. Maria often felt isolated, watching her peers go to school and talk about their futures, while hers seemed confined to survival. The burden of being the eldest daughter in a low-income family meant that Maria had to grow up faster than she wanted to. She missed out on the carefree aspects of youth, trading them for the harsh realities of adulthood. Yet, through it all, Maria remained resilient, driven by her love for her family and her desire to see them through difficult times.

Shonna's Experience in the United States

Shonna, the eldest daughter in a high-income family in the United States, lived a life that was remarkably different from Maria's. Her parents were both professionals, earning comfortable salaries that allowed them to provide Shonna and her siblings with a stable and nurturing environment. Education was a top priority in their household, and Shonna was encouraged to focus solely on her studies and extracurricular activities.

Unlike Maria, Shonna didn't have to worry about contributing to the family's income. Her responsibilities were more aligned with her personal growth—excelling academically, participating in sports, and preparing for college. The pressure Shonna faced was the kind that comes with high expectations for success, but it was free from the economic stress that burdened families like Maria's.

Shonna had access to private tutors, enrichment programs, and opportunities to travel, all of which broadened her horizons and prepared her for a future full of possibilities. Her role as the eldest daughter was centered on being a role model for her younger siblings in terms of academic achievement and personal development. She was expected to set a high standard, but the support system around her made this role feel like an opportunity rather than a burden.

Religious Influences on Personal Freedoms

Religion and community significantly impact the duties and obligations of eldest daughters. In many religious settings, the eldest daughter is often seen as a moral and spiritual guide for her siblings. Religious beliefs can also impose stringent behavioral standards on eldest daughters, reinforcing traditional gender roles and expectations. However, these influences can vary significantly across different communities and levels of religiosity. Here are stories that illustrate the impact of religion in shaping eldest daughters' lifestyles and motivations.

Hana's Dual Role as a Custodian of Faith and Family

Hana, the eldest daughter in a devout Muslim family in Indonesia, grew up with a strong sense of duty that extended far beyond the usual household chores.

From a young age, Hana learned the importance of religious practices such as daily prayers, fasting during Ramadan, and the teachings of the Quran. Her parents, deeply rooted in their faith, relied on Hana to pass these traditions down to her siblings.

Hana's role wasn't just about teaching rituals; it also involved instilling the values of kindness, humility, and respect that were core to their faith. She often found herself mediating disputes between her siblings using the principles she had learned from her own religious education. Her influence was a blend of older-sister affection and spiritual mentorship, a combination that shaped her siblings' understanding of their faith and their behavior in the family and community.

However, this dual role came with its challenges. There were moments when she struggled to maintain an image of perfection and avoid failure, since this would cause her parents and siblings to disapprove of her. Hana's sense of self-worth rested on the reputation she had earned in her family of being morally upright and inspirational. It took courage for her to find an identity outside the leadership role she played at home and allow herself sometimes to be the goofy and laid-back girl she was inside.

Rachel's Balancing Act Between Faith and Ambition

In New York, Rachel, the eldest daughter in a Jewish Orthodox family, faced a different set of challenges as she navigated the intersection of religious obligations and personal aspirations. Growing up in a tight-knit Orthodox community, Rachel was acutely aware of the expectations placed on her as the eldest daughter. She was seen not only as a role model for her younger siblings but also as a bearer of the family's religious values.

As Rachel grew older, she developed a strong interest in pursuing a career in law—a path that excited her, but also posed significant challenges within her religious framework. The demands of her legal studies often conflicted with her religious obligations, and Rachel had to navigate the delicate balance between staying true to her faith and achieving her professional goals. There were times when she had to make difficult choices, such as missing out on important career opportunities because they clashed with religious holidays or Sabbath observance.

Rachel's journey was a constant negotiation between the values instilled in her by her family and community and her own desires for personal and professional fulfillment. Her story highlights the complexities that many eldest daughters face in religious families, where the expectations of faith and the pursuit of individual goals often intersect. Her ability to balance these aspects of her life serves as an inspiration to other eldest daughters who are striving to forge their own paths while staying connected to their cultural and religious heritage.

Finding Pathways to Overcome Eldest Daughter Pressures

Resilience is the ability to recover from setbacks and keep going, even when times are tough. Practicing resilience involves staying positive and developing a mindset that embraces challenges as opportunities for growth. There are many ways that eldest daughters can practice resilience to overcome the heavy burdens they encounter. Here are stories that display positive coping strategies.

Rebecca's Path to Personal Freedom

Growing up in a traditional family, Rebecca was always expected to adhere to the values and paths laid out for her. However, she felt a growing desire for independence and self-discovery that clashed with her family's expectations. She realized that to truly understand herself and find her own happiness, she needed to step out of her comfort zone. After much contemplation, Rebecca decided to pursue higher education in a city far from home, away from her family's immediate influence.

This decision was not without its challenges. Rebecca had to navigate the emotional weight of guilt for making a decision that could bring disappointment to her family. She faced moments of doubt and loneliness, but she embraced these as opportunities for growth. Living independently allowed her to explore her passions, build new relationships, and discover a sense of freedom she had never known before. Her journey was marked by a series of personal milestones that highlighted her resilience and determination.

Emma's Journey to Setting Boundaries

Emma always found herself in the role of the family mediator, tasked with resolving conflicts and managing the needs of her younger siblings. This role, while intended to be supportive, gradually took a toll on her emotional well-being. The constant pressure to be the problem-solver left her feeling overwhelmed and exhausted, and she began to realize that this dynamic was unsustainable.

Determined to find a better balance, Emma decided to practice setting clear boundaries. She started with small, manageable steps such as setting specific times when she would be available to help with family issues and communicating her own needs and limitations to her family.

Initially, this shift was met with resistance and confusion from her loved ones, who were accustomed to her taking on more than her fair share. Yet, Emma remained patient and consistent, gently reinforcing her new boundaries and explaining her need for personal time and space.

Over time, her efforts began to pay off. Her family gradually adapted to the changes, and Emma found herself with more energy and emotional resilience. She learned how to manage her responsibilities more effectively and even grew to improve her relationships within the family.

Sarah's Support Network

Sarah grew up in a large family where she often felt isolated despite being surrounded by people. As the eldest daughter, she was expected to manage family responsibilities while navigating her own personal challenges. The burden of these expectations left her feeling disconnected and stressed, and she struggled to find a support system that could help her cope.

During her college years, Sarah found a turning point when she joined a women's support group on campus. Although initially hesitant, she soon discovered that the group offered a sense of community and understanding that she had been missing. The friendships and mentorship she received from the group provided her with emotional support and practical advice on managing her stress and balancing her family obligations with her personal goals.

Through this external support system, Sarah learned valuable strategies for resilience, such as self-care practices and stress management techniques. She gained new perspectives on her challenges and found solace in the shared experiences of others. The support group became a crucial part of her life, helping her navigate the complexities of her role as an eldest daughter while pursuing her own aspirations.

Adult Sibling Shenanigans: Tales From the Front Lines

Navigating sibling relationships as adults often involves balancing responsibility with the occasional dose of humor. As the eldest daughter, you've likely experienced moments where sibling dynamics blend into heartwarming adventures.

The Holiday Cooking Catastrophe

When the family decided to host Thanksgiving dinner, Claire, the eldest, was tasked with managing the cooking. Her younger brother,

Alex, who had just started experimenting with culinary arts, offered to help. His "secret" ingredient in the mashed potatoes turned out to be way too much garlic, resulting in a dish that could've doubled as a vampire deterrent. Despite the culinary mishap, Claire and Alex spent the evening laughing over takeout and reminiscing about past holidays.

Lesson learned: It's the shared experiences that make family gatherings memorable, even if the food isn't gourmet.

The DIY Home Improvement Fiasco

When Lisa, the eldest, decided to tackle a DIY home improvement project—installing a new light fixture in her living room—she enlisted her younger sister, Nadia, for moral support. What was meant to be a quick upgrade turned into a hilarious evening of mismeasured wiring, a temporary blackout, and an unexpected call to the electrician. Nadia documented the chaos with photos, turning it into a running joke among the siblings.

Lesson learned: Sometimes, the best memories come from the things that don't go as planned, and a good laugh can make even a DIY disaster a bonding experience.

The Impromptu Weekend Getaway

During a spontaneous weekend getaway, Emma, the eldest, was tasked with organizing the trip for her siblings. Her plan suffered a mix-up with the booking dates, leading to a fully booked cabin and a last-minute scramble for accommodations. The siblings ended up in a quirky bed-and-breakfast with mismatched furniture and eccentric decor. Instead of letting the situation ruin the trip, they embraced the adventure and spent the weekend creating inside jokes and making the best of their "unique" lodging.

Lesson learned: Flexibility and a positive attitude can turn travel mishaps into memorable experiences.

The Surprise Birthday Party Faux-Pas

For Mark's 30th birthday, his eldest sister, Laura, planned a surprise party with a guest list she accidentally sent to the wrong email addresses. The result was a mix of surprised and confused faces when a random assortment of people showed up, including a few of Mark's old college friends who hadn't seen him in years. Instead of feeling embarrassed, Laura and Mark rolled with the punches, enjoying an unexpectedly fun and diverse gathering.

Lesson learned: Embracing the unexpected and finding humor in the situation can make any event more enjoyable.

The Family Tech Support Marathon

When their parents' old computer started acting up, Emily, the eldest, was enlisted as the family tech support expert. Her younger brother, Jake, who thought he could help, suggested a series of increasingly complicated "fixes" that only made things worse. The situation escalated into a marathon of troubleshooting calls, online tutorials, and a lot of facepalming. Despite the chaos, the siblings spent the evening cracking jokes about their tech mishaps and reminiscing about their childhood adventures.

Lesson learned: Even in the midst of technological trials, the camaraderie of working through challenges together can turn a stressful situation into a bonding experience.

These stories reflect the unique and often amusing experiences that come with adult sibling relationships, offering a reminder that even grown-up siblings can find joy in shared laughter and cherished memories.

Concluding Thoughts

In this chapter, we've journeyed through the varied experiences of eldest daughters from different cultural, socioeconomic, and religious backgrounds. We have also learned how different women demonstrated resilience to mitigate the pressures of their various family roles. Their stories emphasize the importance of seeking external support and embracing personal growth despite family expectations, reminding us that while the path may be fraught with challenges, there is immense strength and potential in each eldest daughter's journey.

In the next chapter, we explore how eldest daughters can redefine the meaning of success and create new legacies that prioritize personal aspirations alongside family obligations.

*"Our deepest wishes are whispers of our authentic selves.
We must learn to respect them.
We must learn to listen."*

Sarah Ban Breathnach

Chapter 9

Success, Redefined

Balancing Personal and Family Aspirations

Growing up as the eldest daughter usually involves taking on roles that are meant to be shared among different family members. You become the caretaker, the responsible one, and in many cases, the mini adult. These responsibilities shape your idea of success, which then becomes synonymous with meeting the expectations of your family. But what if you could redefine this notion of success?

Success metrics, also known as key performance indicators (KPIs) describe the criteria that let you know when you have accomplished your objectives. These metrics are outlined before you start executing your goals to help you gain a sense of direction and understand what's expected of you.

When you were a young girl, your parents were the ones who outlined the success metrics for becoming a responsible, confident, and healthy adult woman. They taught these metrics to you through sharing their beliefs, establishing rules, and emphasizing certain goals that you needed to strive for. The only trouble with the success metrics laid out by your parents is that they described things that were important to them and not necessarily connected to who you are and how you desire to live your life.

Now that you are an adult, you get to redefine these success metrics according to your core values, beliefs, interests, ambitions, and sense of "right and wrong." One way to do this is by broadening the definition of success to include personal achievements, joy, and contentment.

Instead of focusing solely on traditional benchmarks like career advancements or family approval, consider what brings you genuine happiness. Did you always want to learn a creative pursuit? Can you carve out time to practice that hobby? When personal goals and aspirations form part of your success metrics, they add layers of richness to your life.

The Benefits of Changing What Success Means to You

Rethinking what success means can liberate you from predefined trajectories. Often, eldest daughters follow a "safe path": Graduate from college, get a stable job, buy a piece of property, and maybe even support the family financially. While these are commendable goals, they may not necessarily align with your personal aspirations. Allowing yourself the freedom to redefine success opens up new possibilities. It enables you to explore alternate careers, interests, and lifestyles that you might have previously considered impractical or unachievable.

Your personal aspirations need equal consideration when defining success. Think about what you wanted as a child before the weight of responsibility altered your trajectory. Perhaps you dreamed of traveling, starting a business, or engaging in community service. Allocating time and resources to these dreams can be life changing. When your personal aspirations are given the same weight as family responsibilities, you achieve a balance that nurtures both your family roles and individual essence.

Furthermore, evolving personal goals contribute significantly to life satisfaction. What you wanted five years ago might differ from what you desire today, and that's okay. Adaptability in personal goal-setting is vital. For instance, you might have initially aimed for a high-paying job to support your family. However, as time progresses, you might realize that job satisfaction and work-life balance hold more value for you. Prioritizing evolving goals can mitigate feelings of guilt, leading to greater emotional and psychological well-being.

Consider the journey of an eldest daughter, Keisha, who once saw herself only through the lens of her family's needs. She worked hard, excelled academically, and landed a prestigious job. Yet, something felt amiss. Keisha's personal ambitions, such as writing a novel and learning French, were stifled by her obligations. By rethinking success, she decided to take evening classes in French and reserved weekends for writing. Slowly, her sense of fulfillment grew. Her achievements didn't just resonate with external validations but also echoed within her soul.

Imagine another scenario where an eldest daughter, Iman, chose a less traditional path. Despite initial resistance from her family, she pursued a career in art rather than medicine. Over time, Iman gained recognition and found immense personal satisfaction. By defining success on her terms, she combined personal joy with professional accomplishments, illustrating that unconventional choices can also lead to meaningful success.

Revisiting and evolving your personal goals is a dynamic process. Regularly reflect on your aspirations. Are they aligned with who you are today? Do they bring you joy? Adjustments aren't just acceptable; they are necessary for continued growth and satisfaction. The very act of revisiting your goals allows you to measure growth, not just by achieved targets but by the joy and contentment they bring.

Creating a Vision Board for Success

Visualizing goals and aspirations can inspire action and help you stay focused on your personal objectives. This process begins with the powerful tool of creating a vision board, which is more than just an arts-and-crafts project—it's a tangible representation of what you truly desire in life.

A vision board serves as a constant reminder of your deepest wishes and goals. By placing images, words, and symbols that represent these aspirations on a board, you create a physical manifestation of your dreams. Every time you glance at it, you are reminded of what you want to achieve. This visual cue keeps your goals at the forefront of your mind, helping you prioritize them amidst the many responsibilities that come with being an eldest daughter.

Additionally, a vision board fosters a proactive mindset toward achieving personal goals. Having a clear picture of what you wish to accomplish can be incredibly motivating. It shifts your thinking from passive daydreaming to active planning. This proactive approach encourages you to take concrete steps toward realizing your aspirations. For instance, if your vision board has pictures of a career milestone, seeing it daily might prompt you to seek out educational opportunities or network within your industry to move closer to that goal.

Consistent reminders of your ambitions reinforce your commitment to personal aspirations. In the hustle and bustle of daily life, it's easy to get sidetracked by immediate obligations and forget long-term goals. But a vision board acts as a touchstone; a daily nudge to stay on track. When you place your vision board in a prominent location such as your bedroom or office, it becomes an unavoidable reminder of what you're working toward. This repeated visualization can instill a sense of urgency and dedication, ensuring that you remain steadfast in your pursuits despite external pressures.

Visualization also primes your brain for success by creating neural patterns that make the real-life execution of your goals feel more attainable. The act of visualizing your success—seeing your goals as already achieved—can trigger positive emotions and a sense of accomplishment even before you reach them. This mental rehearsal can boost your confidence and prepare you mentally for the future. For example, envisioning yourself having open communication with your parents about your limits can reduce the anxiety you feel about initiating this discussion and can also improve the outcomes of your discussion when the time comes.

A Step-by-Step Guide to Creating Your Vision Board for Success

Creating a vision board is a straightforward process that can yield significant benefits. Here are simple instructions to follow when designing your board.

Step 1: Collect the Materials

Begin by gathering materials that resonate with your goals. Collect magazines, print images from the internet, or even use personal photographs. Quotes, affirmations, and other text elements that inspire you can also be included. Your selections should evoke a strong emotional connection, as this will deepen your commitment to your goals.

Step 2: Decide on a Theme

Next, select a specific focus or theme for your vision board. Whether it's career advancement, relationship building, or personal growth, having a central theme will help streamline the creation process and ensure that your vision board remains coherent and purposeful. For example, if you aim to advance professionally, include images of your desired job role, office space, and motivational quotes about leadership and success.

Step 3: Arrange the Creative Elements on Your Board

Once you have your materials and theme, arrange them on a board in a visually appealing manner. Start by arranging the elements in a collage layout to see how the final board will look like. When you are satisfied, take some glue and stick the elements in the appropriate places. The layout should be both inspiring and meaningful, as the process of creation is just as important as the final product. Take your time to thoughtfully place each element, allowing yourself to engage deeply with your goals and aspirations.

Step 4: Find a Location

After your vision board is complete, display it strategically. Choose a location where you'll see it regularly—perhaps next to your mirror, above your desk, or in another high-traffic area. Regular exposure to your vision board will continually reinforce your commitment to your goals and keep them vivid in your mind. Each time you pass by, let it serve as a prompt to evaluate your actions and decisions, ensuring that they align with your larger objectives.

Periodically revisit and reflect on your vision board. As life progresses and circumstances change, your goals may evolve. Adjust your vision board as needed to ensure it remains a dynamic and relevant source of inspiration.

This ongoing engagement with your vision board makes it a living document of your aspirations, one that grows with you and adapts to your changing desires. Reflecting on your progress can also highlight the milestones you've reached, providing a sense of achievement and encouraging further effort.

Creating New Family Legacies: Paving the Way for Future Generations

The role of the eldest daughter in a family is often accompanied by a set of expectations that can feel heavy. This pressure may stem from cultural norms, family traditions, or personal beliefs within the family, all of which have been explored throughout the book. These responsibilities can sometimes become overwhelming and create a cycle where burdens are passed down from one generation to the next. You have the ability to redefine how your family serves one another.

To do this, you will need to use the influence you have among your loved ones to promote positive and healthy family dynamics. It starts with you reimagining what family means to you and what values can create an environment that is more supportive and understanding. Once you have figured this out, your job is to convince your family members to adopt this ideal dynamic through showing them its benefits and patiently teaching them the new family framework for future generations.

Below are a few examples of positive behaviors that can help your family create a new and improved family legacy.

Being the Big Sis Your Siblings Can Look Up To

Modeling positive behaviors is a key part of building healthier family dynamics. This means that the way you act can influence others—especially those who look up to you, like younger siblings. When you demonstrate good habits, you're not just helping yourself but also teaching them important lessons. For example, if you take time out for self-care activities such as exercising or reading, your younger siblings might start to see the value in looking after their own well-being. This can lead them to develop their own routines that prioritize their health, both physically and mentally.

One critical aspect of role-modeling is effective stress management. Life can be stressful, and how you handle stress can impact those around you. If you show healthy ways to cope with stress, such as talking about your feelings or practicing mindfulness, your siblings can learn from these examples. They may pick up on your techniques and apply them in their own lives. For instance, if you have a stressful day at school but respond by taking a walk or meditating, they might find this approach helpful when they face their own stressors. This helps create a culture of open communication surrounding mental health and how to manage it.

This silent form of teaching, where actions speak louder than words, is powerful. You don't have to sit down and give a lecture; instead, your everyday behaviors can convey strong messages. Consider the little things you do, like how you treat others or how you handle disappointments. When your siblings see you respond to challenges with resilience and a positive attitude, they are likely to adopt similar behaviors. They might learn to face their own difficulties with courage, knowing that struggles are a part of life and that it's okay to ask for help when needed.

By being a positive role model, you also create a safe space for your siblings to express themselves. Encouraging open discussions about feelings and challenges can help them feel comfortable sharing their thoughts. It's important to listen to them without judgment. If they see you practicing empathy and understanding with others, they will likely mirror this behavior. For instance, if your friend is upset and you take the time to listen and support them, your siblings will learn how to be good friends as well. This can lead to stronger bonds and healthier interactions in their own relationships.

You can also share your experiences in a way that makes it clear that you are still learning and growing. When you talk about your struggles or mistakes, this can help demystify the idea of perfection. It shows that everyone makes mistakes and that it's okay to fail, as long as you learn from it. For example, if you share a story about a time you didn't achieve a goal and how you dealt with it, your siblings may find it easier to cope with their own disappointments. They are likely to appreciate your honesty and be encouraged to try again despite setbacks.

In terms of self-care, leading by example is invaluable. Make it a point to involve your siblings in healthy activities. Whether it's cooking a nutritious meal together, going for a hike, or practicing yoga, these shared experiences can provide both enjoyment and education. You can talk to them about why these activities are important for health and well-being, helping them see self-care as a lifestyle rather than a chore. These moments can be fun, and they help form habits that they can carry into adulthood.

The impact of your role-modeling can extend beyond your family, too. The behaviors you exhibit in your household influence how your siblings interact with peers and other adults outside the home. For instance, if you often show kindness and respect, they will likely take these values into their friendships and other relationships. They may become advocates for positive behavior in their own right, spreading kindness and understanding beyond just family dynamics.

Teaching Your Family How to Become Empathetic Communicators

Effective communication within a family is essential for building strong relationships. It goes beyond just talking; it involves understanding and expressing emotions in a way that is clear and compassionate. Teaching family members how to communicate their feelings effectively can significantly reduce misunderstandings. When people learn to express themselves, resentment tends to fade, and a supportive atmosphere can grow in its place.

For example, let's consider a family where one member often feels unheard. This can lead to frustration and anger over time. However, when that person learns to articulate their feelings, they can start a conversation about how they feel without blaming anyone.

The aim is to create an environment where everyone feels safe to voice their concerns. This practice can start simply by sharing your own emotions and worries. For instance, you might say, "I've been feeling overwhelmed by work lately." This opens up the floor for others to share their feelings, too.

Encouraging open dialogue about feelings is important. It's not always easy to speak about emotions, especially in a family setting where patterns may have been established over the years. To cultivate a culture of open communication, try scheduling regular family check-ins. Set aside some time where everyone can gather to talk about their week and share how they are feeling. This time can be as informal as a dinner gathering or a sit-down session on weekends. The key is to create a relaxed atmosphere where everyone knows they can speak their mind without judgment.

During these discussions, it's crucial to model the kind of communication you want to see. Show your family how to listen as well as how to share. Listening is an active process, and you can demonstrate this by maintaining eye contact, nodding in understanding, and responding thoughtfully to what someone else says. For example, if a family member talks about a tough day at school, rather than just saying "I understand," ask questions like, "What made it so difficult?" This encourages deeper conversations and helps family members feel valued.

When someone shares their feelings, acknowledging those emotions without trying to fix the situation is key. You might say, "It sounds like you had a really hard time." This shows that you understand and care about their experience. It opens up space for emotions to be expressed and starts dismantling any longstanding patterns of miscommunication.

In addition, teaching family members to express emotions in a healthy way is very valuable. There are various techniques that can help in this regard. For instance, using "I" statements can clarify feelings without placing blame. Instead of saying, "You never listen to me," you can phrase it as, "I feel ignored when conversations focus on others." This change makes a significant difference in how messages are received. When family members feel empowered to communicate openly, they will likely have fewer misunderstandings and create stronger connections with each other.

Introducing Your Family to Bonding Rituals and Traditions

Creating strong family bonds is essential for promoting a healthy family dynamic. One effective way to nurture these connections is by introducing the practice of family meetings, where each member of the family has an opportunity to speak about important issues or thoughts they may have. This environment is designed to be safe, allowing everyone to express their opinions and feelings without fear of judgment.

"Mental health check-ins" are another tradition that could be held weekly, where each family member shares how they are feeling emotionally. It could be as simple as asking everyone to rate their week on a scale of one to ten and explain why they chose that number. This encourages everyone to think about their own emotional state and share it with others. These check-ins serve as ongoing reminders that mental health is important and that they can help identify any issues before they escalate. When family members are aware of each other's feelings, they can offer support and understanding.

Moving beyond individual well-being, planning monthly outings dedicated to personal growth activities can be a fun and engaging way to bond as a family. These outings can focus on various wellness activities such as exploring nature trails, participating in yoga classes, or even volunteering together at a local charity. Each month could feature a different activity that promotes not just fun, but also learning and growth.

For instance, if you decide to go hiking, it offers both physical exercise and an opportunity to connect with nature. You can even take the time to discuss the beauty of the environment around you or the importance of conservation. This shared experience will create lasting memories and instill a sense of teamwork and shared values among family members.

Furthermore, scheduling regular family days centered on wellness practices helps normalize the discussion around self-care. It does not have to be elaborate; perhaps it could be as simple as a Saturday morning where everyone participates in a family cooking session. This can educate you all about nutrition while also making it enjoyable to work together. After cooking, you could sit down as a family to enjoy the meal and reflect on what you've learned. Activities like this emphasize the importance of taking care of oneself both physically and mentally, while reinforcing the idea that family can be a source of support and joy.

By replacing older, more rigid family norms with these bonding rituals, you help to create an atmosphere where exploration and individual fulfillment are encouraged. Each family member can explore their personal interests and passions while knowing they have the unwavering support of their family. Moreover, your loved ones can feel a sense of belonging and understanding, which is crucial in strengthening your family unit.

The key is to make these practices part of your family's routine and lifestyle. By doing so, they become cherished traditions that everyone looks forward to and appreciates. Remember also that every family is different, and what works for one may not work for another. Therefore, it's beneficial to remain flexible and adapt these practices to fit your family's unique needs and interests.

Encouraging Your Loved Ones to Seek Professional Help

Sometimes, despite our best efforts, we cannot bring about the positive changes we want in our family on our own. There are moments when it becomes necessary to seek external help. Professional support from therapists or counselors can provide the guidance needed to facilitate important conversations and bring healing within your family unit.

When emotions run high or when issues seem too complex to handle, professionals can offer structured support. They provide unbiased opinions that can help families navigate their emotional challenges. For example, a therapist might help identify patterns of behavior that have developed over many years in your family, and simultaneously offer techniques to change them.

If your family faces long-standing issues or deeply rooted behaviors, the need for professional guidance becomes even more evident. It could be a history of poor communication, unresolved conflicts, or unhealthy patterns that your family members have carried through generations. A professional can act as a neutral party in these situations, helping your family break down barriers that might feel overwhelming when addressed alone. They can introduce tools and strategies that promote effective communication, empathy, and understanding. For instance, a counselor might teach some of your family members how to express their feelings clearly, which fosters better understanding and lessens frustration.

Understand that not every family member will recognize the need for change at the same time. Some may be resistant or unaware of the unhealthy dynamics present in their relationships. Accepting this reality can be liberating. It allows you to focus on your personal growth rather than feeling burdened by the need to convince others of their need for growth.

In this context, building assertiveness becomes vital. When you communicate clearly what behaviors you will no longer tolerate, it creates an opportunity for healthier interaction. Setting boundaries becomes a practical way to explain the consequences of continuing harmful behaviors. For instance, if a family member constantly criticizes your lifestyle choices, expressing your discomfort can stop this cycle and promote healthier communication.

The aim of seeking help and making these changes is to create a new family legacy—one centered around emotional wellness and self-discovery, diverging from traditional roles that may have limited personal growth or happiness. You have the power to shift how your family operates. Modeling positive behaviors and encouraging open communication can set a new tone for future generations.

The Eldest Daughter Bucket List: Things You Deserve to Do for Yourself

The Eldest Daughter Bucket List is a playful yet empowering collection of experiences and activities designed to help you reconnect with yourself, nurture your passions, and enjoy some much-deserved "me time." These are things that might have taken a backseat while you were busy being the rock for everyone else—now, it's *your* turn to shine and have some fun.

Challenge yourself to choose at least one bucket list item to do each month; however, the more items checked off, the merrier!

- **Solo spa day extravaganza:** Treat yourself to a full day of pampering at a spa. Enjoy a massage, facial, and relaxation time with no interruptions. You deserve to be the one receiving care for a change.

- **Weekend getaway to a dream destination:** Plan a spontaneous trip to a place you've always wanted to visit, even if it's just for a weekend. Embrace the adventure, explore new surroundings, and recharge your spirit without any obligations weighing you down.

- **Creative workshop or class:** Sign up for a workshop or class that piques your interest, like pottery, painting, or dance. Allow yourself to explore your creative side without any pressure—just pure enjoyment.

- **Unplugged day of digital detox:** Take a full day to disconnect from your phone, email, and social media. Spend time doing what makes you happy, whether it's reading a book, going for a hike, or simply lounging around without any distractions. This is your day to recharge without any digital noise.

- **Splurge on a "Just Because" gift:** Buy yourself something you've always wanted but never allowed yourself to indulge in: a beautiful piece of jewelry, a luxurious handbag, or that gadget you've been eyeing for months. You deserve it—no special occasion needed.

- **Try an adrenaline-pumping activity:** Step out of your comfort zone and try something adventurous like skydiving, zip-lining, or rock climbing. It's time to prove to yourself that you can conquer anything—and have a blast in the process!

- **Host a "No Responsibility" day with friends:** Invite your closest friends over for a day of fun with no responsibilities—think movies, games, takeout, and lots of laughter. Let the day be about unwinding and enjoying each other's company without any "to-dos."

- **Start a personal journal or blog:** Begin writing down your thoughts, dreams, and reflections in a personal journal or start a blog. It's a space just for you to express yourself freely, document your journey, and celebrate your growth.

- **Attend a concert or live event:** Go to a concert, play, or live event that excites you. Let the music or performance sweep you away and enjoy the thrill of being part of something vibrant and energizing.

- **Take a "Do Nothing" vacation:** Plan a vacation where the sole purpose is to do absolutely nothing—no sightseeing, no schedules, just pure relaxation. Lounge by the pool, nap whenever you want, and savor the luxury of not having to be "on" for anyone.

This bucket list is about giving yourself permission to prioritize your happiness, explore your passions, and enjoy life on your own terms. As an eldest daughter, you've given so much to others; now it's time to invest in yourself. So go ahead, make these experiences your own, and remember that you're not just a caregiver, problem-solver, or role model—you're also someone who deserves joy, fulfillment, and a little bit of indulgence.

Concluding Thoughts

In this chapter, we looked at the unique challenges faced by eldest daughters and the importance of redefining success to balance personal aspirations with family obligations. By broadening the definition of success to include personal joy and achievements, eldest daughters can find fulfillment beyond traditional benchmarks. We discussed the need for self-compassion, the power of visualization through vision boards, and the role of setting boundaries and modeling positive behaviors in establishing healthier family dynamics.

Embracing your desires, whether through creative pursuits, spontaneous activities, or self-care routines, allows you to inspire a family legacy rooted in emotional wellness and mutual support. By prioritizing your own needs alongside family responsibilities, you pave the way for a new generation of eldest daughters to thrive with resilience and self-compassion.

In the final chapter, you will be asked to reflect on your life's journey as an eldest daughter and consider long-term personal growth strategies that you can integrate into your daily life.

*Courage doesn't always roar.
Sometimes courage is the little voice at
the end of the day that says,
"I will try again tomorrow."*

Mary Anne Radmacher

Chapter 10

The Art of Reflection

Get to Know Yourself Better Through Self-Assessments

Reflecting on your journey is an important process that can lead to personal growth and self-awareness. When you take the time to think about your past experiences and the choices you have made, you begin to see how these elements have contributed to the person you have become.

For many, self-reflection is not just a casual thought; it is a deep dive into past events and decisions. This can be particularly illuminating for someone in a position of responsibility within a family, such as the eldest daughter, since the role often comes with various expectations that can clash with personal dreams and desires.

When reflecting, consider the specific moments in your life where family obligations may have taken precedence over your personal goals. Acknowledging these moments is the first step in understanding how family dynamics shape personal choices. You may find it helpful to write these experiences down, as journaling can clarify your thoughts. By outlining what you felt during those times and what you ultimately chose to do, you can start to see the underlying patterns in your decision-making.

As the eldest daughter, you might feel the weight of expectations from your parents and younger siblings. It's essential to ask yourself whether these expectations align with your values and aspirations. Doing so can help you gauge how much of your energy is devoted to meeting others' needs versus pursuing your own. Through this kind of introspection, you can begin to uncover how these dual responsibilities influence your identity and well-being.

Reflect on how you have managed to juggle these competing demands. For instance, did you find creative ways to align family expectations with your personal goals? Or did you struggle to find a compromise, leading to feelings of resentment or unfulfillment? Noticing these patterns allows you to understand yourself better and may even inspire changes in how you prioritize your time and responsibilities.

Another way to engage in self-assessment is to create a list of your core values and compare them to what you currently practice in your life. For example, if independence is a core value for you, are you allowing yourself the freedom to make personal choices? Or are you often swayed by the needs of your family? A values list can serve as a reminder of what is most important to you, helping you make decisions that honor your own aspirations. This can be a liberating experience, as it enables you to develop a clearer sense of self.

Once you have identified areas where family expectations conflict with your personal goals, you may want to consider your options moving forward. Discussing your feelings with family members can be an effective way to bridge an understanding between all of you. You might set aside some time for an open and honest conversation about your aspirations and the responsibilities you feel burdened by. This could lead to a more balanced dynamic where family support aligns with your personal growth.

Reflection Questions to Explore Different Parts of Your Life

In times of reflection, it's important to recognize and celebrate your achievements as well. Consider keeping a success journal where you note down every milestone, big or small. This could include academic accomplishments, personal projects, or even emotional breakthroughs. The act of writing them down can help solidify your growth and remind you of the potential within you, which can sometimes be overshadowed by family duties.

Here are a few reflection questions that can help you examine the role you play in your family and how this important role can positively integrate with other aspects of your life:

1. What roles and responsibilities have I taken on that I never consciously chose? Do these roles align with who I am today, and if not, how can I start redefining them?

2. How do I feel when I put my own needs aside to prioritize others? Am I content, resentful, exhausted, or something else?

3. In what areas of my life do I feel the most pressure to be perfect? How can I begin to embrace imperfection and be kinder to myself in these areas?

4. How do I typically handle conflict within my family or social circles? Is my approach serving me well, or could I benefit from setting healthier boundaries or communicating differently?

5. What are the unspoken expectations I feel from my family, and how do they affect me? Are these expectations realistic or fair? What would happen if I communicated my own needs and limitations?

6. How do I define success for myself, and how much of that definition is influenced by others' expectations? What would success look like if I defined it entirely on my own terms?

7. How do I balance being a role model with being authentically myself? Are there areas where I feel like I'm not being true to myself because of this role? How can I better align my authenticity with being a positive influence?

8. What does self-care look like for me, and how often do I engage in it? Is there a gap between what I need and what I allow myself to do? How can I bridge that gap?

9. When was the last time I did something purely for my own joy or fulfillment? What prevents me from doing this more often, and how can I incorporate more of these moments into my life?

10. Who in my life supports me in prioritizing my well-being, and how can I lean on them more? Am I allowing myself to receive help and support from others, or do I feel I have to do everything on my own?

Setting Positive Future Intentions

Imagining a future where your needs and aspirations come first is powerful. Many eldest daughters often feel the pressure to prioritize others, neglecting their own desires and goals in the process. Shifting your perspective is not just beneficial; it can change your life. By focusing on what you want and need, you open the door to a more fulfilling existence.

To start, it's important to set small, achievable intentions that put your well-being front and center. For instance, you might choose to set aside a few hours each week for a hobby you love. These small commitments can be rewarding and help you reconnect with your passions. As these smaller goals start to feel more integrated into your life, you can gradually expand your intentions.

You might decide to look into furthering your education, whether it's taking a class related to your current job or exploring something new altogether. Changing careers could be another step—researching fields that interest you, networking with professionals, or even attending job fairs. Building new relationships outside your family circle might also be fulfilling. Consider joining clubs or groups that align with your interests, as these could lead to meaningful connections.

Understand that setting intentions is not a one-and-done task. Instead, it should be viewed as a continuous practice that grows and adapts with you. Life will present challenges, and setting guidelines for yourself throughout these ups and downs helps to define your path. Think of them as signposts that keep you on track toward a more balanced and satisfying life.

Another helpful strategy is to share your intentions with friends or mentors you trust. Discussing your plans with supportive people can provide motivation and accountability. When others believe in your ability to create positive change, it boosts your confidence to stick to your goals. Rather than feeling pressured by strict plans, remember that setting intentions is about laying a groundwork where real changes can flourish.

Intention-setting can also be thought of as a flexible process. It's wise to revisit and adjust your intentions periodically because, as life changes, so do you. This means that what you want and need may shift, too. Thus, allowing yourself to adapt your intentions helps to ensure they remain relevant and encouraging.

Reflecting on your past experiences can also be beneficial. Think about the successes you've had and celebrate even the smallest milestones. By recognizing your progress, you boost your morale, and when things don't go as expected, it's also an opportunity to collect feedback and look closely at what could have gone differently. Each experience contributes to your understanding and ability to show compassion toward yourself. Understand that personal growth is not a straight path; it's often marked by both victories and lessons learned.

Beginning with small, manageable intentions can lay a solid foundation for future growth. As you build upon these small steps, you can explore larger goals, always keeping your well-being in mind.

Speak Up: Continue Sharing Your Experiences With Others

Reflecting on your journey as an eldest daughter involves recognizing the unique challenges and responsibilities that come with this role. One significant aspect of this reflection is understanding and discussing

Eldest Daughter Syndrome in broader societal contexts to build awareness and understanding.

Raising awareness about EDS is an essential step in bringing the conversation into the public domain. Sharing knowledge about this phenomenon can help others recognize the patterns and pressures faced by eldest daughters. By highlighting these experiences, you can begin to do your part in destigmatizing the challenges you and many other eldest daughters face, and thus provide validation for many who might be struggling silently.

Parents and family members should also be proactive in creating an environment that recognizes the challenges you encounter as an eldest daughter. By taking the time to acknowledge the hard work that goes into your role, family members can help to ease your burden. Simple gestures like checking in on how you are doing or expressing gratitude for your efforts can make a significant difference. This type of active support can help you feel seen and appreciated.

In addition to family and friends, encouraging an understanding of EDS outside of your immediate family can be just as empowering. Talking about your experiences with friends, coworkers, or peers can extend the conversation. When friends understand what being an eldest daughter entails, they can offer better support or help create a more inclusive environment. Building awareness among your peers also opens more opportunities for dialogue, allowing for greater understanding and empathy in your social circles.

Remember that raising awareness about EDS is not about placing blame. Instead, it is about understanding the unique experiences of eldest daughters and supporting them through their struggles. Every family will have its own unique way of addressing these issues. Some might find that having regular family check-ins works for them, while others might prefer more informal conversations. The important factor is to tailor your approach to what feels right for your family. This can involve creating flexible routines that allow for shared responsibilities or simply making time to listen to each other's concerns.

Society also plays a significant role in promoting awareness of EDS. Educational institutions, media, and community organizations can work together to highlight the difficulties faced by eldest daughters. Schools could incorporate programs to educate students about family dynamics and support systems. Community workshops and seminars can serve as platforms for eldest daughters to share their experiences and coping strategies. These gatherings can spark connections among those who relate to similar challenges.

Support groups can also play an essential part in the conversation around Eldest Daughter Syndrome. These groups offer spaces where eldest daughters can share their experiences with others who truly understand. In a support group, you can talk about your responsibilities and pressures without judgment and find solidarity and comfort in knowing you are not alone. If local support groups are not available, consider looking for online communities where discussions can take place. These forums can also provide useful resources, tips, and guidance to help navigate the challenges faced.

Creating content that raises awareness—like blog posts or social media updates—can also be a powerful way to share your experiences. You might write about specific challenges or share tips on coping mechanisms that have worked for you. This content can reach a wider audience, prompting others to reflect on their situations. It can inspire meaningful conversations and encourage those who may not be aware of EDS to learn more, just like the TikTok video that made #EldestDaughterSyndrome go viral.

Ultimately, the journey as an eldest daughter comes with its challenges, but sharing your experiences leads to greater connection and understanding. Whether through family discussions, support groups, or online communities, the importance of speaking up cannot be overstated. Each voice adds to a growing conversation that can lead to greater awareness and appreciation of the eldest daughter's role. Each time you share your story, you help destigmatize the pressures that accompany this responsibility, paving the way for acceptance and change.

The Eldest Daughter Pledge

The Eldest Daughter Pledge is a reminder to occasionally put yourself first, to embrace your perfectly imperfect self, and to find joy in the little moments that make life meaningful. These pledges are deeply meaningful commitments you can make to yourself, designed to help you cultivate habits that enhance your happiness and well-being. By taking these pledges, you're not only acknowledging the unique challenges of being an eldest daughter but also celebrating the strength, resilience, and love that define who you are.

I Pledge to Embrace Imperfection

I vow to let go of the need for everything to be perfect and to celebrate the beauty of imperfection in myself and others. Mistakes are just opportunities for growth and laughter!

I Pledge to Delegate Without Guilt

I commit to sharing responsibilities with others and asking for help when needed without feeling guilty or overwhelmed. Teamwork makes the dream work!

I Pledge to Celebrate My Wins

I will take time to acknowledge and celebrate my achievements, both big and small, with joy and pride. Every success deserves a little celebration!

I Pledge to Prioritize "Me Time"

I promise to set aside regular moments for myself, whether it's a quiet coffee break, a bubble bath, or a solo walk in the park. My well-being deserves this time!

I Pledge to Laugh Often

I will seek out humor and laughter in my daily life, whether through a comedy show, a funny book, or time spent with loved ones. Laughter is the best medicine!

I Pledge to Set Boundaries With Kindness

I promise to establish and maintain healthy boundaries in a way that is both firm and compassionate. Respecting my limits helps me be my best self.

I Pledge to Seek Joy in the Everyday

I will find and cherish the little moments of joy in daily life, whether it's a funny meme, a delicious treat, or a heart-to-heart with a friend. Happiness is often in the small things!

I Pledge to Nurture My Passions

I vow to make time for activities and hobbies that spark joy and passion in my life. Pursuing what I love enriches my soul and keeps me inspired.

I Pledge to Connect With My Tribe

I will make an effort to build and maintain meaningful relationships with people who uplift and support me. Surrounding myself with positive influences enhances my well-being.

I Pledge to Enjoy the Journey

I commit to embracing life's journey with all its twists and turns, savoring the experiences and learning from them. Life is an adventure, and I'm here for the ride!

These pledges are more than just promises; they are a declaration of your right to live a life that is balanced and fulfilling. So go ahead, make these pledges, and take a step toward a happier, healthier you.

Concluding Thoughts

As you reflect on your journey as an eldest daughter, recognize the intricate balance you've navigated between family obligations and personal aspirations. This chapter has encouraged you to conduct a self-assessment, examining how these roles have shaped your identity and influenced your choices. By asking critical questions and confronting the tension between duty and desire, you've started to uncover patterns that may have held you back from fully embracing your true self. This reflection is not meant to induce guilt but to provide clarity and insight, paving the way for meaningful change.

Looking forward, envisioning a future where your needs and goals take precedence can be a powerful step toward personal growth. Setting realistic intentions and gradually realigning your actions with your inner desires will bring you closer to a balanced and fulfilling life, and sharing your journey with trusted friends or mentors can offer valuable support and accountability.

Remember, this process is ongoing, adapting as your needs evolve. Embrace the journey ahead with compassion and resilience, knowing that prioritizing yourself ultimately enriches all aspects of your life, including your relationships with loved ones.

Conclusion

As we draw this book to a close, it's essential to revisit the journey we've undertaken together. Each chapter has unveiled unique facets of the eldest daughter syndrome (EDS), shedding light on the intricate web of responsibilities, expectations, and unspoken pressures that shape the lives of eldest daughters all over the world.

From the early chapters, we learned about the heavy burden that eldest daughters feel from a young age. Their position in the family hierarchy often means that they take on caregiving roles, sometimes sacrificing their own needs to ensure the well-being of siblings and the smooth running of the household. This "second mom" role, while developing a sense of maturity and reliability, can also lead to burnout and a struggle to establish an identity separate from family obligations.

As we moved through the book, we discussed the emotional labor that eldest daughters frequently undertake. This invisible workload includes managing the family's emotions, mediating conflicts, and providing emotional support. These tasks, though unseen, are significant and can lead to high levels of stress and fatigue. Understanding this aspect of their lives is crucial for recognizing the full scope of their contributions and the emotional toll it can take on their mental health.

In examining identity struggles, we highlighted how eldest daughters often wrestle with perfectionism and the need to meet family and societal expectations. This constant striving for perfection can create immense pressure, leading to anxiety and self-doubt. Recognizing these patterns allows eldest daughters to work toward understanding that it's okay not to be perfect and finally accept who they are. They deserve the same compassion and understanding they offer to others.

Setting boundaries has emerged as a critical theme throughout this book. Many eldest daughters find it challenging to say no or to prioritize their own needs, leading to an overwhelming sense of responsibility. Learning to set healthy boundaries is essential for their well-being. It involves acknowledging their limits, communicating their needs, and ensuring they have time for self-care. By doing so, they can maintain their mental and emotional health while still being supportive family members.

As you reach the end of this journey, take a moment to acknowledge the strength, resilience, and love you bring to the role of the eldest daughter. It's not an easy path—being the one who others look up to, the one who carries so much on her shoulders, and the one who often puts others' needs before her own.

My hope is that through these pages, you've found not only a better understanding of yourself but also a renewed sense of empowerment to prioritize your own well-being. You deserve to live a life that is as full and rich as the love and care you so willingly give to others. It's okay to ask for help or to take time for yourself. It's okay to let go of perfection and embrace the beautifully imperfect journey that is uniquely yours.

Remember, you are more than your role in the family—you are a whole person with dreams, desires, and a life worth living on your own terms. As you move forward, I encourage you to carry the lessons, stories, and strategies from this book with you. Use them as tools to navigate the challenges, but also as reminders of your incredible worth.

The discussion about EDS shouldn't end with this book. It's vital to keep the conversation going. Normalize your experiences by sharing your stories and engaging in dialogues within your communities. Whether it's at a family gathering, a social event, or online, your voice can contribute to creating a culture of understanding and empathy. The more we talk about these challenges, the less isolated eldest daughters will feel.

By sharing your story, you not only validate your experiences but also pave the way for others to come forward with theirs. Your narrative can inspire, comfort, and support other eldest daughters who may be struggling silently. Realizing that they are not alone in their experiences can provide immense relief and encouragement.

If you find that the pressures and stresses of being an eldest daughter are affecting your mental health, don't hesitate to seek support from a therapist or counselor. Professional guidance can offer strategies for managing stress and nurturing your well-being.

As you move forward, I hope you feel empowered to break free from the invisible chains of obligation that have bound you for so long. I hope you find the courage to live your life on your own terms, and the compassion to forgive yourself when you falter. Most of all, I hope you remember that you are not alone.

Thank you for taking this journey with me. If you have found the content contained in this book valuable, please leave a review and comment on the book's Amazon page. Your vote of confidence allows other eldest daughters to easily find this resource and embark on a similar empowering journey.

About the Author

Jaylee Wade is a UK-born writer and educator who knows a thing or two about being the eldest daughter. As the big sister to two younger brothers, she's been navigating the ups and downs of family dynamics her whole life. Her experiences through these roles—both personally and professionally—are what inspired her to better understand the unique pressures on eldest daughters.

With a background in teaching and years spent working with kids, Jaylee's seen firsthand how birth order can shape our emotions and development. Her experiences as a mom have only deepened her understanding of family relationships and the expectations often placed on girls in leadership roles.

Now, as a full-time writer, Jaylee focuses on creating books that help kids thrive emotionally. Her mix of personal experience and professional know-how makes her a relatable and insightful guide for eldest daughters looking to balance their own needs with the responsibilities they carry.

In her latest book, Jaylee brings together personal stories, research, and practical advice to help eldest daughters reclaim their sense of self and navigate the complex expectations of their role.

References

Abudi, D. (2011). Chapter two. The family: Arab society in miniature. *BRILL EBooks.* https://doi.org/10.1163/ej.9789004181144.i-336.11

American Psychological Association. (2017). What is cognitive behavioral therapy? https://www.apa.org/ptsd-guideline/patients-and-families/cognitive-behavioral

Andreev, I. (2024, August 22). *Lifelong learning.* Valamis. https://www.valamis.com/hub/lifelong-learning

Ban Breathnach, S. (n.d.). *A quote by Sarah Ban Breathnach.* A-Z Quotes. https://www.azquotes.com/quote/669296

Burgess, E. W. (2009). The transition from extended families to nuclear families. In *Process of aging: Social and psychological perspectives.* Routledge. https://www.taylorfrancis.com/books/edit/10.4324/9781315127460/process-aging-david-popenoe

Burnout. (n.d.). Psychology Today. https://www.psychologytoday.com/za/basics/burnout

Cherry, K. (2024, April 3). *Navigating the challenges of eldest daughter syndrome.* Verywell Mind. https://www.verywellmind.com/eldest-daughter-syndrome-8623347#toc-the-psychological-impact

Clarke, J. (2023, May 5). *How narrative therapy works.* Verywell Mind. https://www.verywellmind.com/narrative-therapy-4172956

Des Marais, S. (2022, November 10). *The importance of play for adults: Tips for being more playful.* Psych Central. https://psychcentral.com/blog/the-importance-of-play-for-adults

Elizabeth Bennet. (n.d.). Charactour. https://www.charactour.com/hub/characters/view/Elizabeth-Bennet.Pride-and-Prejudice

Fletcher, J. (2023, November 14). *How to validate yourself.* Psych Central. https://psychcentral.com/health/ways-to-validate-yourself

Focused Labs. (2023, September 5). *Unleashing your dreams: The power of vision boards.* Medium. https://medium.com/get-focused/unleashing-your-dreams-the-power-of-vision-boards-d8ed6983d011

Gates, M. (2023, October 16). *Two-thousand-and three powerful voices luncheon.* Bill & Melinda Gates Foundation. https://www.gatesfoundation.org/ideas/speeches/2003/10/melinda-french-gates-2003-powerful-voices-luncheon

The Growth Catalysts Team. (2024, May 9). *Embracing uniqueness: Celebrating individuality and authenticity.* ESOFT Lifelong Learning. https://esoftskills.ie/embracing-uniqueness/

Hamilton, D. R. (2022, January 27). *The science of affirmations.* Dr David R Hamilton. https://drdavidhamilton.com/the-science-of-affirmations/

Huffington, A. (n.d.). *A quote by Arianna Huffington.* BrainyQuote. https://www.brainyquote.com/quotes/arianna_huffington_396029

Iheme, A. (2020, July 9). *Giving to yourself: Self-forgiveness.* Medium. https://amandaiheme.medium.com/giving-to-yourself-self-forgiveness-ac5479575557

Kayata, E. (2024, April 24). What is eldest daughter syndrome? Is it a real condition? *Northeastern Global News.* https://news.northeastern.edu/2024/04/24/eldest-daughter-syndrome/

Keller, H. (n.d.). *A quote by Helen Keller.* Goodreads. https://www.goodreads.com/quotes/3443-when-one-door-of-happiness-closes-another-opens-but-often

Kirshenblatt, M. (2014, April 11). *Sansa stark is a strong female character*. Matthew Kirshenblatt. https://matthewkirshenblatt.ca/2014/04/11/sansa-stark-strong-female-character/

Kuo, J. R., Fitzpatrick, S., Ip, J., & Uliaszek, A. (2022). The who and what of validation: an experimental examination of validation and invalidation of specific emotions and the moderating effect of emotion dysregulation. *Borderline Personality Disorder and Emotion Dysregulation, 9*(1). https://doi.org/10.1186/s40479-022-00185-x

Laderer, A. (2024, July 18). *What is eldest daughter syndrome?* Charlie Health. https://www.charliehealth.com/post/eldest-daughter-syndrome

Lansford, J. E. (2022). Annual research review: Cross-cultural similarities and differences in parenting. *Journal of Child Psychology and Psychiatry, 63*(4), 466–479. https://doi.org/10.1111/jcpp.13539

Leno, M. (2024, May 23). *A psychologist's take on "eldest daughter syndrome."* Psychology Today. https://www.psychologytoday.com/us/blog/mind-matters/202405/a-psychologists-take-on-eldest-daughter-syndrome

The Lisa Simpson: Read like an INFJ personality. (n.d.). Mango Publishing. https://mangopublishinggroup.com/the-lisa-simpson-read-like-an-infj-personality/

Luthria, K. (2024, May 2). 'Eldest daughter syndrome': What is it and why is everyone talking about it right now?. *The Guardian*. https://www.theguardian.com/culture/2024/may/02/eldest-daughter-syndrome-viral-tiktok-trend

Michael, A. (n.d.). *A quote by Adrian Michael*. Pinterest. https://in.pinterest.com/pin/322500023299101686/

Miller, B. (2024, March 20). New study reveals fresh evidence for 'eldest daughter syndrome.' *Independent*. https://www.independent.co.uk/life-style/health-and-families/eldest-daughter-syndrome-study-new-evidence-b2515755.html

Moore, S. (2024, May 17). *15 best motivational songs of all time*. SingersRoom. https://singersroom.com/w48/best-motivational-songs-of-all-time/

Najumi, M. (n.d.). *A quote by Mohadesa Najumi*. Goodreads. https://www.goodreads.com/quotes/988725-the-woman-who-does-not-require-validation-from-anyone-is

Obama, M. (n.d.). *A quote by Michelle Obama*. BrainyQuote. https://www.brainyquote.com/quotes/michelle_obama_791345

Parisette-Sparks, A., Bufferd, S. J., & Klein, D. N. (2017). Parental predictors of children's shame and guilt at age 6 in a multimethod, longitudinal study. *Journal of Clinical Child and Adolescent Psychology*, 46(5), 721–731. https://doi.org/10.1080/15374416.2015.1063430

Perry, E. (2023, August 8). *The meaning of personal values and how they impact your life*. BetterUp. https://www.betterup.com/blog/meaning-of-personal-values

Radmacher, M. A. (n.d.). *A quote by Mary Anne Radmacher*. Goodreads. https://www.goodreads.com/quotes/38657-courage-doesn-t-always-roar-sometimes-courage-is-the-little-voice

Raypole, C. (2019, March 8). *How schema therapy can help you undo harmful patterns*. Healthline. https://www.healthline.com/health/schema-therapy

Rozycki, A. (n.d.). *Superwoman? Yes I am*. Mental Health Match. https://mentalhealthmatch.com/articles/stress/superwoman-yes-i-am

Rutledge, P. (2016, January). *Everything is story: Telling stories and positive psychology*. Research Gate. In *Gregory, E. M., & Rutledge, P. B.* Exploring Positive Psychology: The Science of Happiness and Well-Being. ABC-Clio Publishers. https://www.researchgate.net/publication/343921003_Everything_is_Story_Telling_Stories_and_Positive_Psychology

Sandberg, S. (2013, July 7). *A quote by Sheryl Sandberg*. Goodreads. https://www.goodreads.com/quotes/749772-we-cannot-change-what-we-are-not-aware-of-and

Sandell, R. (2021, November 24). *Katara's character arc in "Avatar: The Last Airbender" is the most inspiring*. Collider. https://collider.com/avatar-the-last-airbender-katara-character-explained/

Shah, B. (2022, May 20). *How can rewriting your narrative help you gain closure?* Book Therapy. https://www.booktherapy.io/blogs/news/how-can-rewriting-your-narrative-help-you-gain-closure

Shahid, M. (2023, June 8). *Eldest daughter syndrome: Growing up in a South Asian household*. Artefact. https://www.artefactmagazine.com/2023/06/08/eldest-daughter-syndrome-growing-up-in-a-south-asian-household/

Stone, E. (n.d.). *A quote by Emma Stone*. Goodreads. https://www.goodreads.com/quotes/10536490-i-can-t-think-of-any-better-representation-of-beauty-than

Success metrics. (2024). Service Design Tools. https://servicedesigntools.org/tools/success-metrics

Thinking Focus. (2023, October 13). *Imposter syndrome: The unseen barrier to success*. LinkedIn. https://www.linkedin.com/pulse/imposter-syndrome-unseen-barrier-success-thinkingfocus-warxe/

21 most motivating songs about growth to help your life - public domain music. (2024, July 8). Public Domain Music. https://www.pdmusic.org/songs-about-growth/

Varghese, M., Kirpekar, V., & Loganathan, S. (2020). Family interventions: Basic principles and techniques. *Indian Journal of Psychiatry*, *62*(2), 192–200. https://doi.org/10.4103/psychiatry.indianjpsychiatry_770_19

von Furstenberg, D. (2014). *A quote by Diane von Furstenberg*. Goodreads. https://www.goodreads.com/quotes/8123944-love-is-about-relationships-yet-the-most-important-relationship-is

Walker, A. (n.d.). *A quote by Alice Walker*. Goodreads. https://www.goodreads.com/quotes/15083-the-most-common-way-people-give-up-their-power-is

WebMD Editorial Contributor. (2024, March 5). *Burnout: Symptoms and Signs*. WebMD. https://www.webmd.com/mental-health/burnout-symptoms-signs

What is burnout? (2022, February 1). Cleveland Clinic. https://health.clevelandclinic.org/signs-of-burnout

White, G. (2021, November 20). *Firstborn African Daughter Syndrome*. Medium. https://medium.com/ayaba-legacy/firstborn-african-daughter-syndrome-142e8d910c5

Williams, J. M. (2023, June 27). *Curiosity is your superpower: How to become a lifelong learner*. Medium. https://medium.com/dear-family/curiosity-is-your-superpower-how-to-become-a-lifelong-learner-8ca5eeb6fe37

Printed in Great Britain
by Amazon